———— IN ————

GOD'S
IMAGE

A Study of the Nature of Man

IN
GOD'S
IMAGE

A Study of the Nature of Man

CHAD RAMSEY

GOSPEL
ADVOCATE
A TRUSTED NAME SINCE 1855

Copyright © 2013 by Gospel Advocate Co.

IT IS ILLEGAL AND UNETHICAL TO DUPLICATE COPYRIGHTED MATERIAL.

All scripture quotations, unless otherwise indicated, are taken from the New King James Version®. Copyright © 1982 by Thomas Nelson, Inc. Used by permission. All rights reserved.

All rights reserved. No part of this publication may be reproduced, stored in a retrieval system or transmitted in any form or by any means – electronic, mechanical, photocopy, recording, or any other – except for brief quotations in printed reviews, without the prior permission of the publisher.

Published by Gospel Advocate Co.
1006 Elm Hill Pike, Nashville, TN 37210
www.gospeladvocate.com

ISBN 10: 0-89225-591-9
ISBN 13: 978-0-89225-591-7

DEDICATION

To my parents, Glenn B. and Judy Ramsey.

Thank you for bringing me up "in the training and admonition of the Lord" (Ephesians 6:4).

And to Beverly, whose love and support are priceless (Proverbs 31:10).

TABLE OF CONTENTS

1   *What Is Man?* 9

2   *A Physical Being* 15

3   *A Spiritual Being* 23

4   *An Intellectual Being* 33

5   *A Social Being* 41

6   *An Ethical Being* 49

7   *A Privileged Being* 59

8   *A Sexual Being* 67

9   *A Freewill Being* 77

10   *An Emotional Being* 87

11   *A Religious Being* 95

12   *A Mortal/Immortal Being* 103

13   *A Hopeful Being* 111

     Afterword 119

     Glossary 121

     Endnotes 123

1

What Is Man?

"What is man that You are mindful of him, And the son of man that You visit him?" (Psalm 8:4). When those words were written, the psalmist was pondering the vastness of the universe. As he considered the complexities of creation, he wrestled with the idea that man, in comparison with all of God's magnificent works, seems small and unimportant. Despite this seeming insignificance, however, he recognized that God showed interest in the well-being of humanity.

The question of man's position is one that has been considered throughout the ages of time. Is man a creature who owes his existence to chance? Is he perched precariously atop the evolutionary chain? Or does man exist intentionally? And if man exists intentionally, what role was he created to fill? Along with these questions, any thorough discussion of man's nature must also address his composition. Is man an animal? Or is he more than a highly developed physical specimen?

A study of the nature of man will lead the honest student into a variety of fields. To answer questions about man's physical nature, he must look closely at the origin of our universe; to answer questions about man's spiritual nature, he must delve deeply into what it means to be created in God's own image (Genesis 1:27). A study of man's nature will address social issues such as the importance of fellowship. It will address ethical issues. And ultimately, it will focus upon the question raised in Job 14:14: "If a man dies, shall he live again?"

Historical Perspective

Not surprisingly, mankind has long been concerned with man's nature. This fascination can be traced in secular history at least as far back as the Greek philosopher Protagoras (c. 490–420 B.C.). Protagoras is best known for this statement: "Man is the measure of all things: of things which are, that they are, and of things which are not, that they are not." [1] And while the exact meaning of this statement is debated, the assessment of William F. Lawhead seems reasonable:

> Two interpretations have been given of this slogan: (1) each individual person provides his or her own standard for implementing things, or (2) society as a whole is the measure of all things. Under either interpretation, he expresses a radical humanism and relativism that says there is no standard other than those that individuals or societies invent. Actually, Protagoras seems to have embraced both alternatives ... he affirmed an individualistic subjectivism with respect to perception and a social subjectivism with respect to ethics. [2]

Regardless of whether Protagoras had the individual man or human race in mind, his assessment promotes *relativism* and leaves little room for absolute truth (words throughout the text that are in bold, italic type may be found in the glossary on page 121).

In stark contrast to Protagoras' view of man, Solomon's assessment, found in the book of Ecclesiastes, serves to reject relativism and promote submission to God. Having searched for life's meaning in various self-gratifying ventures, Solomon concluded his treatise with these words: "Let us hear the conclusion of the whole matter: Fear God and keep His commandments, For this is man's all. For God will bring every work into judgment, Including every secret thing, Whether good or evil" (Ecclesiastes 12:13-14). Whereas Protagoras assigned to man the place of prominence, Solomon reserved that position for

God. Instead of man (whether individually or collectively) having the ability to determine for himself what is true, Solomon emphasized that it is God who must be obeyed.

According to Solomon, life's meaning is not found in man's wisdom (Ecclesiastes 1:16-18), pleasure (2:1-3), possessions (vv. 4-11), popularity (4:13-16), ambition (6:3-9), or ability (9:10-12). Instead, life's meaning is found in the respectful obedience of the one who recognizes that he or she exists for the purpose of seeking the Lord. [3] Rather than being the measure of all things, man therefore is *measured* by the One who created all things.

Man's Nature

Establishing man's position under the authority of God in no way diminishes the position he occupies in the created realm. He was, as Psalm 8:5 notes, created "a little lower than the angels." Nevertheless, God "crowned him with glory and honor." The record of man's exaltation above the physical creation is found in Genesis 1:26-30. In this text he is given dominion over both the plant and animal kingdoms. And this dominion, according to the text, was awarded because man was created in the very image of God.

But what does it mean to be created in God's image? The comments of noted 19th-century commentator Adam Clarke are worthy of consideration:

> [Man's soul] was made in the *image* and *likeness* of God. Now, as the Divine Being is infinite, he is neither limited by parts, nor definable by passions; therefore he can have no *corporeal image* after which he made the body of man. The image and likeness must necessarily be intellectual; his mind, his soul, must have been formed after the nature and perfections of his God. The human mind is still endowed with the most extraordinary capacities; it was more so when issuing out of the hands of the Creator. God was now producing a spirit, and a spirit, too, formed after the perfections of his own nature. God is the fountain whence this spirit issued, hence the stream must resemble the spring which produced it. God is holy, just, wise, good, and perfect; so must the

soul be that sprang from him: there could be in it nothing
impure, unjust, ignorant, evil, low, base, mean, or vile. [4]

In essence, man is not *just* a physical being. He is composed of both
body *and* spirit.

The idea that man is a twofold being is not limited to Scripture.
French philosopher René Descartes (1596–1650) drew this conclusion
upon purely rational grounds. Longing to find some truth that he could
recognize as certain, he sought to systematically doubt everything he
believed to be true. Ironically, this very process led Descartes away
from skepticism. He reasoned: "I was persuaded that there was nothing in all the world, that there was no heaven, no earth, that there
were no minds, nor any bodies: was I not then likewise persuaded
that I did not exist? Not at all; of a surety I myself did exist since I
persuaded myself of something." [5] In other words, Descartes came to
realize that even if he doubted the existence of everything, he could
not doubt that he – a thinking being – existed. Descartes' thought
process led him to accept that man also possesses a body – a thing
entirely different from the mind. Thus, he concluded that man is
composed of both mind and body.

No doubt the method employed by Descartes to reach his conclusion
was nothing short of brilliant. And although he is often credited with
articulating the idea of mind-body dualism, we must not lose sight of
the fact that this point was stressed in Scripture long before Descartes
set forth the idea. According to Genesis 2:7, the body of the first man
was formed from the dust of the ground, and God "breathed into his
nostrils the breath of life." Man did not become a living being without
both a physical body and the soul provided by God (see Zechariah 12:1).
The apostle Paul emphasized the duality of man when he wrote the
following: "Therefore we do not lose heart. Even though our outward
man is perishing, yet the inward man is being renewed day by day"
(2 Corinthians 4:16). But perhaps James made the point best of all when
he wrote, "For as the body without the spirit is dead, so faith without
works is dead also" (James 2:26).

Scripture stresses that man has the ability to control both body and
spirit. Emphasizing this, Paul reminded the Corinthians: "For you were

bought at a price; therefore glorify God in your body and in your spirit, which are God's" (1 Corinthians 6:20). Note that Paul did not simply instruct the Corinthians to control themselves; instead, he made a clear statement charging the Corinthians to exercise control over their entire beings – both body and spirit. When we consider the context in which this statement is found – a passage warning the Corinthians to avoid sexual sins – the idea becomes all the more important.

In essence, Paul was saying: Do not just refrain from engaging in sexual sins, but make sure you keep your thoughts under control too. This seems to be the same idea Jesus had under consideration when He said: "You have heard that it was said to those of old, 'You shall not commit adultery.' But I say to you that whoever looks at a woman to lust for her has already committed adultery with her in his heart" (Matthew 5:27-28). Man has the ability and the obligation to control himself both externally and internally.

Conclusion

Given the instructions found in Scripture governing both physical and mental actions, we may conclude that man is clearly a complex being whose characteristics deserve thoughtful consideration. Both experience and revelation teach that man's body will not last forever. The soul, however, is another matter (cf. Ecclesiastes 12:7; Hebrews 9:27). No doubt this is why Jesus issued this warning: "Do not fear those who kill the body but cannot kill the soul. But rather fear Him who is able to destroy both soul and body in hell" (Matthew 10:28). Man is vastly superior to the rest of God's creation; he is woefully inferior to his Creator. Nevertheless, he is faced with the task of utilizing all of his being to glorify the One in whose image he is made (cf. Matthew 22:37).

Why Study About the Nature of Man?

Having established that man is under God's authority and that he possesses both body and spirit, it remains to be seen why such a study is worthy of our time. The short answer is that we should desire to understand man's nature so we can better order our lives to please God. The long answer is that we study the nature of man to gain an understanding of the complexities that make man what he is. Our existence is not just about the physical. Neither is our existence merely about the spiritual. If it were, why would God have placed man in a physical environment? Why not just make spiritual beings, like the angels?

Describing Jesus, Luke wrote, "And Jesus increased in wisdom and stature, and in favor with God and men" (Luke 2:52). In this description we see that our Lord progressed intellectually, physically, spiritually and socially. Therefore, much more exists to man's growth and development than meets the eye, and if Jesus' example teaches us anything, we are challenged to grow and develop in a similar fashion. The purpose of this study is for us to come to a better understanding of how we can do just that. *So what is man?* The answer to this question will consume the rest of our study.

Questions for Consideration

1. Study the context of Psalm 8. What is the meaning of the psalmist's question in verse 4: "What is man that You are mindful of him, And the son of man that You visit him?"

2. What are some of the potential dangers associated with Protagoras' assertion that "man is the measure of all things"?

3. Discuss Solomon's search for life's meaning in the book of Ecclesiastes. Why do people today continue to look for meaning in the same places mentioned by Solomon?

4. What does it mean to be created in God's image?

5. Discuss the dual nature of man. In what way(s) is man different from the rest of God's creation?

6. In what areas did Jesus grow and develop?

2

A Physical Being

A ny discussion about the nature of man must consider, at least, the physical component of man's existence. This will entail taking a closer look at man's material body, examining the origin of that body, and considering its use. It also will include an overview of pertinent biblical passages showing that man is more than just a highly developed animal.

Characteristics of Man's Physical Body

Biologists note that all living things possess "to a greater or lesser degree, the properties of specific organization, irritability, movement, metabolism, growth, reproduction and adaptation." [1] Observation reveals that humans meet these qualifications. In general terms, humans have uniform skeletal structures, respond to stimuli, possess the ability to move from place to place, digest and transform food into energy to be used by the body, give birth to offspring, and adjust to the environment in which they find themselves. Thus, human beings are living beings.

Note that the properties associated with living beings are all subject to verification. That is, they can be *measured*. The apostle John described Jesus with similar terminology when he wrote the following:

> That which was from the beginning, which we have heard,
> which we have seen with our eyes, which we have looked
> upon, and our hands have handled, concerning the Word
> of life – the life was manifested, and we have seen, and
> bear witness, and declare to you that eternal life which was
> with the Father and was manifested to us – that which we
> have seen and heard we declare to you, that you also may
> have fellowship with us; and truly our fellowship is with
> the Father and with His Son Jesus Christ. (1 John 1:1-3)

John did not write simply to affirm Jesus' existence. He described how Jesus could be *heard, seen* and *touched.* John's point is that Jesus was a real physical being!

Man's physical body exhibits marks of design. Aside from possessing characteristics associated with living things, perhaps the most remarkable aspect of the human body is its complexity. A casual glance at any of the various systems that constitute the physical body would reveal marks of design. One who examines the complexities of the circulatory system can hardly conclude a lack of design. For example, the human heart beats an average of 70 times per minute, 60 minutes per hour, and 24 hours per day for a lifetime. During that span, the heart will beat approximately 2.5 billion times – a necessary function that naturally occurs without man ever giving it a single thought.

Even seemingly simple physical components that we often overlook lend themselves to the idea that the human body is the result of intelligent design. Take, for example, human hair. Noting the evidences of design in man's hair, Wayne Jackson wrote:

> Hair has several functions. It is a part of the skin's sentry
> system. Eyelashes warn the eyes to close when dust strikes
> them. Body hairs also serve as levers, connected to muscles,
> to help squeeze the oil glands. Hair acts as a filter in the
> nose and ears. Hair grows to a certain length, falls out, and
> then, in most instances, is replaced by new hair. Hair is
> "programmed" to grow a certain length. Eyelashes obviously
> do not grow as long as scalp hair. Who planned it this way?
> Clearly there is design in this circumstance. [2]

When considering that the body's systems not only exhibit marks of design but also cooperate with the other bodily systems in a manner that does not disrupt functionality, the evidence pointing to a divine designer becomes all the more prominent. This leads to the same conclusion drawn by 18th-century apologist William Paley in his classic book, *Natural Theology:*

There cannot be a design without a designer; contrivance without a contriver; order, without choice; arrangement, without anything capable of arranging; subserviency and relation to a purpose, without that which could intend a purpose. All these imply the presence of intelligence and mind. [3]

No wonder the psalmist wrote: "I will praise You, for I am fearfully and wonderfully made; Marvelous are Your works, And that my soul knows very well" (Psalm 139:14). **Man's physical body is functional.** The human body is also capable of functioning in an appreciable manner. That is to say, the body that is free from defect can perform certain tasks. The eyes not only serve to decorate the body – they provide sight. The ears not only adorn the sides of a man's head – they receive and distinguish varying sounds. In essence, it could be stated correctly that the eye is capable of seeing and the ear is capable of hearing. Describing this, the wise man wrote, "The *hearing* ear and the *seeing* eye, The LORD has made them both" (Proverbs 20:12, emphasis added). The human eye can, in one instant, function as a sort of telescope by focusing upon a faraway object. In the next instant, the eye can operate as a sort of microscope, focusing upon a minute object. The ability to switch from focusing upon something in the distance to examining an object up close is a wonderful testimony to the functionality of the human eye. Of course, similar things could be said about the rest of man's physical body.

Man's physical body is subject to decay. As wonderful as the human body is, it was not designed to last forever. Paul wrote: "Therefore we do not lose heart. Even though our outward man is perishing, yet the inward man is being renewed day by day" (2 Corinthians 4:16). The author of Hebrews noted that "it is appointed for men to die once, but after this the judgment" (9:27). James likened life to a vapor, describing how it "appears for a little time and then vanishes away" (James 4:14). And Moses reminded us: "The days of our lives are seventy years; And if by reason of strength they are eighty years, Yet their boast is only labor and sorrow; For it is soon cut off, and we fly away" (Psalm 90:10).

Because our physical bodies are subject to various sicknesses and diseases, we are to take care of them. Describing this as a natural thing, Paul wrote, "For no one ever hated his own flesh, but nourishes and cherishes it" (Ephesians 5:29). Proper care would include eating healthy foods (Daniel 1:8-16), avoiding substances and activities that poison and harm the body (1 Corinthians 6:15-19), getting an adequate amount of rest (Mark 6:30-32), and engaging in a reasonable amount of physical activity (1 Timothy 4:8). Nevertheless, we must always keep in mind that our physical health is not nearly as important as our spiritual health (3 John 2).

The Origin of Man's Physical Body

Those who deny the existence of God still recognize that man's existence must be attributed to some source. Subsequently, they argue that all living things came to exist from nonliving matter. What is perhaps most telling about their argument is the fact that they readily admit spontaneous generation *does not occur* today. To account for the existence of living things, however, they must argue that some form of spontaneous generation did occur billions of years ago. Notice the following evolutionary explanation:

> Although the spontaneous generation of life at present is unlikely, it is most probable that billions of years ago, when chemical and physical conditions on the earth's surface were quite different from those at present, the first living things did arise from nonliving material. [4]

It is telling that scientists, whose discipline is supposedly based upon observation, are willing to accept at least three assumptions about processes that cannot be observed in order to propagate the theory of evolution. (1) They must assume that some form of spontaneous generation occurred – despite the fact spontaneous generation has never been observed and modern research (such as that done by Louis Pasteur) has continuously disproved the idea.

(2) They must assume that the earth is billions of years old. The three components of evolution – massive reproduction, genetic variation and natural selection – would necessarily require this length of time in order to occur. To support this claim, scientists argue that modern dating methods show the earth to be quite old. Yet they fail to consider the possibility that the earth was not created in an infantile state. In other words, if the earth was created perfectly aged, the dating methods would be skewed.

(3) They must assume that the conditions on the earth were quite different at the time of supposed spontaneous generation. Again, this assumption is conjecture designed to fit with evolutionary theory. In light of the fact that the assumptions used to support the theory of evolution provide no evidential basis for belief, it is reasonable to reject that proposition.

Dismissing the theory of evolution as untenable, our attention turns to the other viable alternative to man's origin: special creation. Having already established that the human body exhibits marks of design, it is not surprising to find a record of man being designed in Scripture. According to Genesis 2:7, "the LORD God formed man of the dust of the ground, and breathed into his nostrils the breath of life; and man became a living being." The process of forming (or fashioning) man accords with the idea of designing man. The text also sets forth the idea that man is both a physical and spiritual being. Commenting on this, Adam Clarke wrote:

> In the most distinct manner God shows us that man is a compound being, having a body and soul distinctly, and separately created; the body out of the dust of the earth, the soul immediately breathed from God himself. Does not this strongly mark that the soul and body are not the same thing? The body derives its origin from the earth, or as *aphar* implies, the dust; hence because it is earthly it is decomposable and perishable. [5]

Having created man, God then created woman by taking a rib from man's side (Genesis 2:21-22). And from the first created pair, all humans have come by virtue of the reproductive principle whereby everything brings forth after its own kind. [6]

But is the idea of special creation more tenable than evolution? In my estimation, when the evidence of design within the human body is coupled with evidence supporting the veracity of the biblical account of creation, a reasonable basis for belief in special creation results. [7] Thus, the question of man's physical origin is answered by pointing to the God who created all things out of nothing.

The Purpose of Man's Physical Body

When we stop to consider that Scripture describes how man's physical body eventually will return to dust (Genesis 3:19; Ecclesiastes 12:7), we are reminded that the purpose of man's existence is not simply to gratify the flesh. In fact, those who spend their time focusing only upon the physical pleasures of life are doing nothing more than living for a world that is passing away. That is why Peter pointedly wrote, "For we have spent enough of our past lifetime in doing the will of the Gentiles – when we walked in lewdness, lusts, drunkenness, revelries, drinking parties, and abominable idolatries" (1 Peter 4:3). And that is why John reminded his readers that "the world is passing away, and the lust of it; but he who does the will of God abides forever" (1 John 2:17).

So how are we to use our physical bodies? We are to use them to glorify God. Paul described this as he addressed the Corinthians by reminding them about Jesus' sacrifice on the cross and charging them to fulfill their responsibilities as His followers. He wrote: "For you were bought at a price; therefore glorify God in your body and in your spirit, which are God's" (1 Corinthians 6:20). This involves the practice of self-control (9:27) and constant effort (Romans 13:13-14).

Conclusion

Regardless of what else man might be, he is certainly a complex physical being. His body exhibits marks of intelligent design and is completely functional. But man is much more than just a highly developed animal. Rather than being the product of billions of years of evolution, he is a created being who is made in God's image (Genesis 1:27). His essence, then, is not limited to his physical existence, for physical bodies experience decay and eventual death. Instead, man is a physical being with a spiritual purpose; that is, to use both his body and his spirit to glorify God.

Questions for Consideration

1. How does the human body meet the criteria of being a living being?

2. Describe a way, other than those mentioned in the chapter, in which the human body exhibits marks of design.

3. Is the functionality of the human body important? Why or why not?

4. Reread the passages that emphasize the physical body is subject to decay. What should the Christian learn from these passages?

5. Discuss the assumptions upon which the theory of evolution is based. In your opinion, why is the theory so widely accepted?

6. How is the idea of special creation a viable option to the theory of evolution?

7. For what purpose should man use his physical body? Cite Scripture to support your answer.

3

❦

A Spiritual Being

A ddressing His disciples, Jesus asked: "For what profit is it to a man if he gains the whole world, and loses his own soul? Or what will a man give in exchange for his soul?" (Matthew 16:26). A glance at these two pertinent questions reveals that there is more to man than his physical existence. In essence, man has a soul worth more than the whole world. But what is this soul? And why is it so valuable? In hopes of answering these questions, this chapter focuses on the spiritual nature of man. As we study, we will consider the source of man's spiritual nature, discuss the distinctiveness of man's spiritual nature, contemplate the obligations enjoined upon one who possesses a spiritual nature, and remind ourselves of the potential destinations of spiritual beings.

The Source of Man's Spiritual Nature

As James concerned himself with proving that man's faith and works go hand in hand, he illustrated his point by writing, "For as the body without the spirit is dead, so faith without works is dead also" (James 2:26). James was, in essence, drawing a parallel between a living body and living faith. One can no more have a body without a spirit and live than he or she can have faith without works and please God. Although James was not addressing the subject of man's nature specifically, the implication of his statement is still valid. Living beings possess both a physical body and a spirit, and when the spirit departs from the body, the body dies. Recognizing the importance of this duality, 19th-century theologian Charles Hodge remarked:

> The Scriptural doctrine of the nature of man as a created spirit in vital union with an organized body, consisting, therefore, of two, and only two, distinct elements or substances, matter and mind, is one of great importance. It is intimately connected with some of the most important doctrines of the Bible. … It is because of this connection, and not because of its interest as a question in psychology, that the true idea of man demands the careful investigation of the theologian. [1]

Having discussed man's physical nature in the previous chapter, we now turn our attention to man's spiritual nature. Of primary importance to this discussion is the source of man's spiritual nature. So what is the source of man's spirit?

To answer this important question, we must first note the Bible affirms that *God* possesses a spiritual nature. According to John 4:24, "God is Spirit." Therefore, when Scripture affirms that man is made in God's image (Genesis 1:27; Colossians 3:10), it is asserting that man has a spiritual nature, which he received from God and which sets him apart from the rest of creation. This, of course, is why man was placed in charge of the creation at its beginning (Genesis 1:28-30; 2:15). This is also why man is held accountable for his actions. He is not merely a beast who reacts to physical stimuli and desires. Instead, man has the ability to weigh his desires against his duties.

Like Moses, who chose "rather to suffer affliction with the people of God than to enjoy the passing pleasures of sin" (Hebrews 11:25), man can choose to suppress his physical desires as he seeks to please God. At the same time, however, man can also reject God in favor of his own appetite. As Esau chose physical gratification over the physical and spiritual blessing of his birthright (Genesis 25:29-34; Hebrews 12:16-17), so man may turn his back upon God. Nevertheless, because he is made in God's image, man is responsible for his actions. The statement found in Romans 6:23 – "For the wages of sin is death, but the gift of God is eternal life in Christ Jesus our Lord" – was written strictly because man is a spiritual being. Animals do not sin, and they are not proper candidates for the redemption found in Christ. But man, as an individual created in God's image, has both the capacity to sin and the need for redemption.

At what point, then, does man receive his spirit? Given the definition of life provided by James – the body without the spirit is dead – a reasonable conclusion is that an individual obtains his spirit at the same moment his body is conceived. This accords with the idea that the Lord "forms the spirit of man within him" (Zechariah 12:1). Bible commentators C.F. Keil and F. Delitzsch note, "The forming of the spirit within man does not refer to the creation of the spirits of souls of men once for all, but denotes the continuous creative formation and guidance of the human spirit by the Spirit of God." [2] To say it another way, God creates each individual's spirit within his body at the point of conception. Thus, Job argued, "Did not He who made me in the womb make them? Did not the same One fashion us in the womb?" (Job 31:15).

Our conclusion is that man is a spiritual being because he is created in God's image. This, of course, is a wonderful blessing. Man has the capacity to understand, to choose and to love. But at the same time, man is responsible for both his physical and spiritual actions.

The Distinctiveness of Man's Spiritual Nature

When we consider that God is involved in the formation of each individual's spirit and that each individual is made in God's image, we are forced to consider whether the individuals made are identical in nature or unique. Addressing this issue from a philosophical standpoint, C.S. Lewis wrote:

> The signature on each soul may be a product of heredity and environment, but that only means that heredity and environment are among the instruments whereby God creates a soul. I am considering not how, but why, He makes each soul unique. If He had no use for all these differences,

I do not see why He should have created more souls than
one. Be sure that the ins and outs of your individuality are
no mystery to Him; and one day they will no longer be a
mystery to you. The mould in which a key is made would
be a strange thing, if you had never seen a key: and the key
itself a strange thing if you had never seen a lock. Your
soul has a curious shape because it is a hollow made to fit
a particular swelling in the infinite contours of the divine
substance, or a key to unlock one of the doors in the house
with many mansions. For it is not humanity in the abstract
that is to be saved, but you. [3]

While Lewis' argument that God created each individual to fill a
particular need within the divine substance is certainly debatable, [4]
there is merit to his idea that if all individuals were identical, God
would have needed to create only one.

Rather than creating individuals who act and react in exactly the same
manner, God created individuals with a common spiritual nature. Men
and women have the ability to reason, the ability to understand God's
expectations, and the ability either to submit to or to reject God's plan.
Ironically, a quality that makes humans similar also enables them to be
vastly different. That quality is the ability to exercise free will. Thus,
in our quest to determine whether God created individuals identically
or uniquely, we need only look at the reactions of individuals to see
their differences.

For example, Cain and Abel had similar genetic and environmental
influences. Nevertheless, when they offered sacrifices before the Lord,
Abel offered an acceptable sacrifice whereas Cain did not (Genesis
4:3-5). When we consider Hebrews 11:4, which states Abel's sacrifice
was more excellent than his brother's because it was offered by faith,
we notice an undeniable spiritual difference in the brothers. This does
not mean Cain had to reject God's wishes, for he did not. The passage
does, however, illustrate the point that although all men are made in
God's image, they possess the ability to act and react very differently.

God has made man in His own image, but He has not forced man
to behave in any particular manner. When we sin, it is because we

choose to do so, not because we lack the capacity to avoid sinful actions. Emphasizing this point and highlighting the unique nature of each individual, James wrote:

> Blessed is the man who endures temptation; for when he has been approved, he will receive the crown of life which the Lord has promised to those who love Him. Let no one say when he is tempted, "I am tempted by God"; for God cannot be tempted by evil, nor does He Himself tempt anyone. But each one is tempted when he is drawn away by his own desires and enticed. Then, when desire has conceived, it gives birth to sin; and sin, when it is full-grown, brings forth death. (James 1:12-15)

Man's Obligations as a Spiritual Being

God has placed certain obligations upon man because of his nature. Some of these obligations are physical, as evidenced by this command: "Be fruitful and multiply; fill the earth and subdue it" (Genesis 1:28). But many more of these obligations are based upon man's existence as a spiritual being. So what are some obligations God requires of man?

God requires man to worship. The requirement for worship is not due to a need of God. Paul made this plain when he informed the Athenians that God is not "worshiped with men's hands, as though He needed anything, since He gives to all life, breath, and all things" (Acts 17:25). From this we can conclude that worship is commanded because it benefits man. But how?

It serves to remind man that One exists who is greater and thus worthy of his praise. It would be easy for man, as the crown jewel of the physical creation, to become self-centered. Worship alleviates this problem by causing man to focus his attention upon God. If we need a reminder as to why we are to turn our attention to God in worship, the psalmist provided three reasons in Psalm 100:3: (1) because He is our master – "Know that the LORD, He is God"; (2) because He is our maker – "It is He who has made us, and not we ourselves"; and (3) because He is our protector – "We are His people and the sheep of His pasture."

Worship requires man to use his entire essence – both body and spirit. Jesus actually made this point when describing proper worship to the Samaritan woman at the well. He said, "God is Spirit, and those who worship Him must worship in spirit and truth" (John 4:24). His insistence upon worshiping in truth requires man to physically engage in actions authorized by Scripture. His insistence upon worshiping in spirit requires man not only to possess the appropriate attitude but also to seek to engage his entire being in the process. Because God is Spirit, it should come as no surprise that those who worship Him acceptably must do so by engaging the spirit created by Him in His own likeness.

God requires man to respect other men. This requirement, like the requirement to worship, is given to man because he possesses a spiritual nature. That nature, and the recognition of its source, is what should motivate man to show ultimate respect for the lives of others. Notice, for example, the foundation for the prohibition of murder in Genesis 9:6: "Whoever sheds man's blood, By man his blood shall be shed; For in the image of God He made man." The idea that murder should be avoided, according to this text, stems from the idea that God made man in His own image. Consequently, man is to live in a manner that shows deep respect for the lives God created (see also 50:15-21). This is not something that can be expected of purely physical creatures. But it is certainly an obligation that creatures possessing a spiritual nature can meet.

In addition, man's respect for other men should reach far beyond the prohibition of murder. Because he recognizes that other men are created with a spiritual nature, man should show respect in the way he speaks and deals with others. James warned his readers that inconsistencies along these lines should not occur: "But no man can tame the tongue. It is an unruly evil, full of deadly poison. With it we bless our God and Father, and with it we curse men, who have been made in the similitude of God. Out of the same mouth proceed blessing and cursing. My brethren, these things ought not to be so" (James 3:8-10). The way in which man deals with his fellow man should be on a higher plane than the kind of interaction found among brute beasts.

God requires man to live in a manner that brings glory to His name. Creatures who possess a spiritual nature are expected to conduct themselves in a manner that reflects positively upon their creator. Whether we consider Jesus' admonition to "let your light so shine before men, that they may see your good works and glorify your Father in heaven" (Matthew 5:16); Paul's charge to live lives that are "holy, acceptable to God, which is your reasonable service" (Romans 12:1); or Paul's reminder that we "were bought at a price; therefore glorify God in your body and in your spirit, which are God's" (1 Corinthians 6:20), clearly man is obligated to live in a way that distinguishes him from the rest of God's creation. This is true, along with the obligations to worship and to show respect to one's fellow man, because man is more than just a physical specimen.

The Destiny of Those Who Possess a Spiritual Nature

What, then, is the benefit of possessing a spiritual nature? Namely, man has the opportunity to live for eternity with God when this world is destroyed (2 Peter 3:10-13). John Mark Hicks has noted:

> The eschatological promise of God is that we will be with him "forever." This is the central hope of God's people, that is, that God will be present among them. To dwell in the house of the Lord forever is the singular hope of God's people, and it is a hope that will find fulfillment when Jesus returns. Then we will see the face of God and dwell with him forever (Revelation 22:1-5). [5]

This, of course, means we really should not be living for the present at all. Instead, we should be longing for that which is to come. After all, it will be a world in which "there shall be no more death, nor sorrow, nor crying" (Revelation 21:4). And when we consider all the difficulty and strife associated with physical life, it is little wonder that possessing a spiritual nature involves the benefit of realizing that our existence encompasses so much more than the struggles of the physical world (see 1 Corinthians 15:19).

Individuals with a spiritual nature have the opportunity to live in preparation for their spiritual reunion with God. No matter what struggles we face in this life, they pale in comparison to the bliss of heaven (Romans 8:18), and when we contemplate how wonderful heaven will be, we begin to understand how Paul could describe man's physical struggle as "our light affliction" (2 Corinthians 4:17).

Each man or woman who lives or has ever lived will spend eternity in either heaven or hell. Because "flesh and blood cannot inherit the kingdom of God" (1 Corinthians 15:50), our eternal destination must be a spiritual place. Either this place will be one of eternal bliss or eternal torment. Our personal destination depends upon our willingness to obey or reject the Savior (see Hebrews 5:9). And it is important to note that "we must all appear before the judgment seat of Christ, that each one may receive the things done in the body, according to what he has done, whether good or bad" (2 Corinthians 5:10). In essence, we are individuals who possess a dual nature: We are spiritual, and we are physical. And when *we* are judged, that judgment will be based upon what *we* did while we inhabited our physical bodies. Man's body may die, but his soul will never die.

Conclusion

Appropriately, we bring this chapter to a close by noting Paul's admonition to the Thessalonians: "Now may the God of peace Himself sanctify you completely; and may your whole spirit, soul, and body be preserved blameless at the coming of our Lord Jesus Christ" (1 Thessalonians 5:23). Existence of the terms "spirit" and "soul" in the same context should cause the reader to take careful notice because these terms often are used interchangeably. Nevertheless, they appear together here.

So what is the difference between the two? Former *Gospel Advocate* Editor Guy N. Woods offered an explanation:

> Our Lord is said to have given his life (*psuchee*, soul) for a ransom (Matthew 20:28), but he gave his *pneuma*, spirit, to God (Luke 23:46). Christ allowed his life (*psuchee*, soul) to be taken, but his crucifiers were not allowed to seize or restrain his spirit. [6]

According to Earl Edwards, Paul likely used these terms in 1 Thessalonians 5:23 "in order to emphasize that his desire was that the totality of each Christian be kept 'without blame,' or just above all censure." [7]

In other words, men, who are living beings, must devote their entire essence – life, spirit and body – to the service of God. As a spiritual being, man must live in view of eternity.

Questions for Consideration

1. How can we know that there is more to man's existence than the physical? Cite Scripture to support your answer.

2. In what way does God's nature (see John 4:24) help us understand the nature of man?

3. What are some examples from the Bible of individuals who chose to deny the world and serve God?

4. What are some examples from the Bible of individuals who chose to deny God and serve the world?

5. Discuss the significance of Zechariah 12:1.

6. How would you reveal, through Scripture, that each individual possesses a unique spirit?

7. Discuss the obligations of man as a spiritual being. Can you think of other obligations not mentioned in the text?

8. How does 2 Corinthians 5:10 show that man is a dual being?

4

An Intellectual Being

The description of Jesus' growth and development, found in Luke 2:52, is revealing: "Jesus increased in wisdom and stature, and in favor with God and men." When we stop to examine the four areas mentioned in this passage, we find that Jesus developed intellectually, physically, spiritually and socially. Regarding this statement, James Burton Coffman wrote, "The true humanity of our Lord is thus brilliantly presented by Luke, no less than his true deity." [1] And while Jesus clearly is set forth in this passage as a man, the passage also helps to define *what* man is. In other words, the areas in which Jesus grew and developed as a human are areas in which all men should grow and develop. Thus, the purpose of this chapter is to consider man as an intellectual being.

Man Is Capable of Thought

The idea that man has the ability to think – that is, to consider, distinguish between, classify, and act or refrain from acting upon various impulses or feelings – rests at the very heart of what distinguishes man from all other physical beings. Rather than merely being programmed to respond to physical stimuli, man is capable of making ethical and moral decisions. Man's ability to think does not only affect how he cares for himself physically; it is intrinsically tied to how he behaves spiritually. Man has the ability to draw conclusions based upon the things he observes, and he has the ability to build upon previously learned material in order to draw *appropriate* conclusions.

The psalmist was doing this very thing when he wrote, "When I consider Your heavens, the work of Your fingers, The moon and the stars, which You have ordained, What is man that You are mindful of him, And the son of man that You visit him?" (Psalm 8:3-4). After examining the vastness of the universe, the psalmist reflected upon God's power and expressed wonder about God's continued interest in mankind. When one realizes this passage is quoted in Hebrews 2:6-8 in a context that concerns itself with the redemptive work of Jesus, it becomes clear the psalmist was not thinking simply about the physical blessings God provides for man.

Man's ability to think is mentioned explicitly in several passages throughout the Bible. The psalmist wrote, "I thought about my ways, And turned my feet to Your testimonies" (Psalm 119:59). This passage illustrates how man's cognitive activity can persuade him to change his behavior in light of alternative information. In this case, the psalmist compared his actions to those prescribed by the testimonies of God and realized a change was needed. Another passage that refers to man's ability to think is 1 Corinthians 13:11 in which Paul wrote: "When I was a child, I spoke as a child, I understood as a child, I thought as a child; but when I became a man, I put away childish things." The explicit reference to thinking "as a child" serves to indicate that man's intellectual capacity increases as he matures.

Note that Scripture also contains passages that reveal man has the ability to think incorrectly. In Genesis 20, Abimelech confronted Abraham and asked why he had identified Sarah as his sister rather than his wife. This was Abraham's response: "Because I thought, surely the fear of God is not in this place; and they will kill me on account of my wife" (v. 11). Another example of incorrect thinking is recorded in 2 Kings 5:11, where we find Naaman's response after he was told by the servant of Elisha to wash in the Jordan River seven times to cleanse his leprosy. He said, "Behold, I thought, He will surely come out to me, and stand, and call on the name of the LORD his God, and strike his hand over the place, and recover the leper" (KJV). In both of these passages, the thinking of the individuals was incorrect. Nevertheless, even the existence of wrong or misguided thinking serves to substantiate the claim that man has the ability to think.

In no passage is man's thoughtfulness challenged more directly than in Isaiah 1:18. Recording the words of the Lord, the prophet wrote: "Come now, and let us reason together." The appeal to man's ability to reason also is found numerous times in the New Testament. In fact, it was common for those who presented the gospel message to reason with their audiences. Paul did this before Felix when "he reasoned about righteousness, self-control, and the judgment to come" (Acts 24:25). These and other passages clearly indicate that God expects man to use his ability to reason – and to do so correctly.

With that being said, we must take heed that we do not place so much confidence in man's ability to reason that we reject things because we lack understanding. John Mark Hicks described this danger by contrasting *Reason* (with a capital "R") and *reason* (with a lowercase "r"):

> The believer, of course, does not reject reason. Biblical reason is rational, that is, it is reasonable and coherent. Believers cannot avoid the use of reason and they should not try. But this is quite different from exalting Reason to a prominence which denies the possibility of mystery or where faith must submit to the lofty demands of Reason. It is also different from exalting Reason to a prominence which denies the possibility of anything which is beyond reason itself. The believer does not view human reason as the ultimate reality. Rather, believers understand that human reason is a finite attempt to understand and comprehend the infinite God. Believers use reason to understand Revelation, but they also accept that Revelation often unveils truths that are beyond reason and reveals a reality beyond our finitude. That is the essential difference between Reason and reason. [2]

So how is man supposed to reason? And are there principles that should govern the way he thinks? Before answering, we should note that the very idea man has the ability to think and reason implies that he has the capacity to judge between items that are true and false. And of course, if man has the ability to distinguish between things that are true and false, then proper thinking and reasoning surely must demand that man only accept what is true and reject what is false. In his book *Logic: An Introduction*, Lionel Ruby wrote, "Every person who is interested in logical thinking accepts what we call the 'law of rationality,' which may be stated as follows: *We ought to justify our conclusions by adequate evidence.*" [3] This does not mean that men will never think irrationally. But it does mean that when men follow the law of rationality, proper thinking occurs. Describing this process, Thomas B. Warren wrote: "When one functions in a rational manner, he says, in effect, to himself, 'the conclusions which I draw must not outrun or be out of harmony with the evidence which is relevant to the truth of the question which I am considering at any given time.' " [4] Clearly, man is capable of thought.

Man Is Capable of Grasping Truth

Foundational to the act of thinking is the existence of truth. This becomes clear when one realizes that thought processes often serve to evaluate and distinguish between the truthfulness or falsity of a particular proposition. If truth does not exist, the thinking process is robbed of moral significance. But if it can be established that truth exists and that man is capable of grasping it, the importance of man's intellect becomes undeniable.

Mankind has long questioned the reality of truth. For example, Pilate, in wrestling with the task of sentencing Jesus, asked, "What is truth?" (John 18:38). The context of John 18 reveals that Pilate was more likely struggling with going against what he perceived to be true than seeking a philosophical definition. Nevertheless, perhaps the question he raised is easier to illustrate than answer. Truth is something you know when you see it.

In describing the difficulty of formulating a precise definition for truth, Roderick M. Chisholm wrote:

It may be, of course, that some ingenious philosopher can formulate an adequate definition of "true" which does not refer to such entities as "states of affairs." But I think it is accurate to say that no philosopher has done so up to now. In the absence of any acceptable alternative, we must resign ourselves to a definition that refers to states of affairs that exist and to states of affairs that do not exist. [5]

Perhaps we might simplify the definition by saying truth is an accurate depiction of reality.

However we seek to define truth, it is impossible for the Christian to define truth apart from either the Word of God or the Son of God. Jesus said: "I am the way, the truth, and the life. No one comes to the Father except through Me" (John 14:6). And Jesus prayed: "Sanctify them by Your truth. Your word is truth" (17:17). James D. Bales expounded upon this idea:

> Jesus is Himself the truth, as well as the teacher of truth (John 14:6). He is the true light in contrast with that which is spurious (John 1:9). In contrast with the law and its system of shadows which came by Moses, grace and truth came by Jesus Christ (John 1:17; Colossians 2:17). God, who sent Christ, is true, and Jesus spoke the truth which the Father taught Him (John 8:26, 28, 40, 45). The truth which Jesus taught was absolute truth, not relative truth. It was truth which could be known by man because Christ revealed it to man. [6]

The important point is that truth – absolute, objective truth – exists. And just as important, man has the ability to know it (John 8:32).

The events recorded in Acts 2 serve to illustrate this point. On that day, a multitude of Jews had gathered in Jerusalem to observe the Pentecost. Upon hearing the apostles speak in their own languages, the Jews expressed their amazement: "Look, are not all these who speak Galileans? And how is it that we hear, each in our own language in which we were born?" (vv. 7-8). Two points of truth are immediately evident: (1) The Jews heard the apostles speak in their own languages, and (2) the Jews recognized that the apostles were native Galileans.

To further illustrate the point that man has the ability to grasp truth, consider that Peter's sermon, rather than appealing simply to the emotions of man, was based squarely upon four facts (or truths). Peter argued (1) that the events transpiring were the fulfillment of Joel's prophecy (Acts 2:16-21), (2) that the Jews could have known Jesus by the miracles He performed (v. 22), (3) that the tomb of Jesus was empty (vv. 29-31), and (4) that eyewitnesses had seen the resurrected Jesus (v. 32). If man is incapable of grasping truth, then the idea of basing an argument on facts is nonsensical. But if man is capable of grasping truth, as proven by the example of the Jews who responded to Peter's sermon (v. 37), then the intellect of man is an important component of his being.

Man Is Capable of Applying Truth

Having already established that man has the capacity to think and having set forth the idea that man has the ability to learn, it remains to be shown that man can use these functions – thinking and learning – to alter his previous course of action. This, of course, is the very thing that occurred when the Jews responded to Peter's sermon on Pentecost. Learning they were guilty of crucifying the Son of God, they considered the ramifications and asked Peter what they could do to make things right: "Men and brethren, what shall we do?" (Acts 2:37). Upon hearing Peter's instructions (v. 38), the Jews "who gladly received his word were baptized" (v. 41).

The ability to apply the knowledge man accumulates is often referred to as wisdom. And wisdom is, according to Scripture, something man can possess. Solomon wrote:

> Get wisdom! Get understanding! Do not forget, nor turn away
> from the words of my mouth. Do not forsake her, and she
> will preserve you; Love her, and she will keep you. Wisdom
> is the principal thing; Therefore get wisdom. And in all your
> getting, get understanding. (Proverbs 4:5-7)

When man is wise, he has the ability to apply the knowledge he has accumulated in the best possible way. He is not merely acting instinctively or responding to stimuli; he is thinking, learning, evaluating and acting upon the basis of available information. His actions can be evaluated as to whether they are ethically or morally good – and it is important to note that he is responsible for those actions.

Conclusion

Because man has the capacity to think, learn and apply things to his life, he is held to a higher standard than the rest of the physical creation. Man's intellect stands as one of his defining characteristics. His ability to experience remorse and regret and his ability to resolve to act differently indicate his intellectual freedom. Because the decisions that man makes can be judged as either good or bad, we may conclude that his intellect is a vital component in his nature. Man, then, is an intellectual being.

Questions for Consideration

1. In what way does Luke 2:52 indicate that man is an intellectual being?

2. What are some of the things involved in the thinking process?

3. What does 1 Corinthians 13:11 teach us about man's intellectual capacity?

4. How does man's ability to think incorrectly reflect upon the idea that man is an intellectual being?

5. Discuss the difference between Reason and reason. When God invites man to reason with Him (Isaiah 1:18), what does He mean?

6. What is "the law of rationality"? Do you believe this law is important? Why or why not?

7. How would you define truth?

8. In what way(s) do the events on Pentecost in Acts 2 illustrate that man is capable of grasping truth?

9. What is wisdom? Why is wisdom important?

5

A Social Being

From the very beginning of man's existence, God recognized man's need for companionship: "And the LORD God said, 'It is not good that man should be alone; I will make him a helper comparable to him' " (Genesis 2:18). As a result, God created Eve from Adam's side. Since that time, man could be described correctly as a social being. Other passages of Scripture laud the benefits of close relationships with others. King Solomon wrote:

> Two are better than one, Because they have a good reward for their labor. For if they fall, one will lift up his companion. But woe to him who is alone when he falls, For he has no one to help him up. Again, if two lie down together, they will keep warm; But how can one be warm alone? Though one may be overpowered by another, two can withstand him. And a threefold cord is not quickly broken. (Ecclesiastes 4:9-12)

These and other passages in the Bible help us to see the importance of interacting with our fellow man. If social interaction is not present, man is robbed of one of his obvious needs, which is why God concluded that "it is not good that man should be alone." Man needs to interact with and associate with others. As George Herbert Livingston put it, "Isolation is unwholesome. By implication, social relationship, i.e., fellowship, is good. Hence God determined to provide man an help meet for him, literally, a helper corresponding to him, one who was equal and adequate for him." [1]

As we consider man as a social being, this chapter will focus on two distinct issues. (1) We will examine why humans need other humans. This discussion will include a close look at the benefits associated with fellowship. (2) We will look at two of the institutions created by God to accommodate man's social needs. Just as Jesus "increased ... in favor with ... men" (Luke 2:52), we also must seek to develop socially. That is not to say we should seek to secure a high social standing for its own sake. Rather, we should seek to develop genuine relationships so we might be aided – and so we might be able to aide others – in our ultimate journey toward heaven.

Why Do Humans Need Other Humans?

Unlike God, man has genuine needs. Some of these needs exist because man is a physical being. Thus, he needs enough food to sustain his body, enough rest to keep his body from becoming ill, and clothing and shelter to keep him from being exposed to the elements. Man also has needs that pertain to his spiritual nature. Chief among them is the need for redemption from his sins. And as can be deduced from God's creation and placement of Eve with Adam, man seemingly has the need to be with other humans.

Apart from Scripture, throughout history individuals often have discussed the value of social interaction. Aristotle (384–322 B.C.), for example, spent a great deal of time describing this benefit as he discussed the city-state. He wrote: "A complete community constituted out of several villages, once it reaches the limit of total self-sufficiency, practically speaking, is a city-state. It comes to be for the sake of living, but it remains in existence for the sake of living well." [2] Aristotle seemingly recognized the important and diverse contributions that various individuals can make to one another's lives. Consequently, he went on to conclude that "anyone who is without a city-state, not by luck but by nature, is either a poor specimen or else superhuman. Like the one Homer condemns, he too is 'clanless, lawless, and homeless.' " [3]

The conclusion drawn by Aristotle regarding the individual separated from the city-state mirrors Cain's response in Genesis 4:13. After being told he would be a "fugitive and a vagabond," Cain exclaimed, "My punishment is greater than I can bear!" Cain's anguish, stemming from his separation from both family and God, indicates that the importance of social interaction has been recognized since the creation of the world. Man certainly was created with the ability to interact with his fellow man. Frederick Copleston observed, "Man's gift of speech shows clearly that nature destined him for social life." [4] Regardless of whatever else might be said in response to Copleston's statement, man's ability to speak does, at least, seem to indicate he is a social being.

But why is social interaction so important? And why can man not live in isolation? To answer these questions, we must remind ourselves about the very purpose for man's existence – the reason God created man – which involves man's willingness to seek God. Paul described this in his sermon on Mars' Hill:

> And He has made from one blood every nation of men to dwell on all the face of the earth, and has determined their preappointed times and the boundaries of their dwellings, so that they should seek the Lord, in the hope that they might grope for Him and find Him, though He is not far from each one of us; for in Him we live and move and have our being, as also some of your own poets have said, "For we are also His offspring." (Acts 17:26-28)

Solomon, making the same point, wrote: "Let us hear the conclusion of the whole matter: Fear God and keep His commandments, For this is man's all" (Ecclesiastes 12:13).

It follows that the purpose of social interaction is to help man be better prepared, by the support of those around him, to fulfill his God-given purpose. In other words, man is more capable of doing God's will when he is encouraged by others than when doing so alone. And if this is correct, then it underscores the importance of involving ourselves in the lives of friends and family members. No wonder Paul wrote the following: "Brethren, if a man is overtaken in any trespass, you who are spiritual restore such a one in a spirit of gentleness, considering yourself lest you also be tempted. Bear one another's burdens, and so fulfill the law of Christ" (Galatians 6:1-2).

To answer the question raised at the beginning of this section, humans need other humans because of the fellowship and support that friends and companions provide. Furthermore, men even benefit by learning from and interacting with those with whom they do not enjoy a close relationship. Nevertheless, at least three benefits associated with genuine fellowship – the kind of fellowship that exists between individuals who seek the best for one another – serve to explain why the social development of man is important.

(1) Fellowship provides comfort in the face of great difficulty. Like Job's friends, who "made an appointment together to come and mourn with him, and to comfort him" (Job 2:11), those interested in the lives of others may seek to ease the burdens of those who struggle. In fact, Christians are supposed to seek to comfort others because they have been comforted by God (2 Corinthians 1:3-4). Whether we do this by being present when one loses a loved one or faces physical challenges, by "strengthen[ing] the hands which hang down" (Hebrews 12:12) through encouraging words or actions, or by petitioning God in prayer for friends and loved ones – something the apostle Paul desired fellow Christians to do for him (Romans 15:30-32) – we may help one another respond to life's trials in numerous ways.

(2) Fellowship provides us with courage and strength. When man is standing alone, like Elijah thought he was in 1 Kings 19:13-14, it is easy to give up or quit; but when man is standing with the support of his friends and brethren, like Peter was on the day of Pentecost (Acts 2:14), he is better suited to accomplish the task at hand. Describing the effect one friend can have upon another, the author of Proverbs wrote, "As iron sharpens iron, So a man sharpens the countenance of his friend" (Proverbs 27:17).

Matthew Henry, 18th-century Bible commentator, explained and commented about the text:

Men are filed, made smooth, and bright, and fit for business (who were rough, and dull, and inactive), by conversation. This is designed, 1. To recommend to us this expedient for sharpening ourselves, but with a caution to take heed whom we choose to converse with, because the influence upon us is so great either for the better or for the worse. 2. To direct us what we must have in our eye in conversation, namely to improve both others an ourselves, not to pass away time or banter one another, but to *provoke one another to love and good works* and so to make one another wiser and better. [5]

(3) Fellowship encourages us either to deny or turn away from sin. When alone, man is not as capable of rejecting temptation as when he is encouraged by others. Thus, the author of Hebrews reminded his readers to "exhort one another daily, while it is called 'Today,' lest any of you be hardened through the deceitfulness of sin" (3:13). Of course, if good companionship can enhance one's ability to shun sin and ungodliness, then bad companionship can have just the opposite effect. Paul so warned, "Do not be deceived: 'Evil company corrupts good habits'" (1 Corinthians 15:33). Given the great influence our friends and associates can have upon us, we should make every effort to surround ourselves socially with those who seek our well-being. As Proverbs 27:6 notes, "Faithful are the wounds of a friend, But the kisses of an enemy are deceitful."

God's Provisions for Man's Social Needs

Having established the benefits associated with man's relationships, we now examine three institutions designed by God for man's social benefit. (1) God created the institution of marriage (and thus the home) when he created woman and gave her to man. He did this, as has already been noted, because "it is not good that man should be alone" (Genesis 2:18). Marriage, then, is God's solution to this problem. Presumably, God recognized that man is better suited to fulfill his ultimate purpose with the institution of marriage than without it. Describing how this is possible, Thomas B. Warren commented:

Marriage is not a relationship whereby the two partners stand with their backs to one another, each using marriage

only for his own selfish purposes. Neither is marriage to
be pictured by two persons facing one another, so that
they worship one another. They are to worship God, not
one another. Instead of these two erroneous views, marriage is better considered as two people standing side
by side facing toward heaven, with the resolve to help
one another to be happy in this life, to help one another
walk closer to God. All of the various aspects of marriage should be pointed toward this goal. Mature people
can help one another to this goal. Immature people will
drive one another away from it. [6]

In addition to companionship, areas in which the home is to function include disciplining its members (Proverbs 22:6; Hebrews 12:9),
educating its members (Ephesians 6:4), making physical provisions for
its members (1 Timothy 5:8), providing exercise for its members (4:8),
and harboring the sexual relationship that exists between husband and
wife (1 Corinthians 7:3-5). It is worth noting that if man lacked the
capacity for social behavior, then the home – and the good accomplished
because of it – would not exist. Thus, the institution of the home exists,
at least in part, because man is a social being.

(2) The government traces its authority for existence to God. Paul
noted: "Let every soul be subject to the governing authorities. For there
is no authority except from God, and the authorities that exist are appointed by God" (Romans 13:1). When we consider that governments
exist for the expressed purpose of punishing those who do evil and
praising those who do good (1 Peter 2:13-14), it becomes clear that the
institution of government is intimately related to man's social nature.
Because mankind forms societies and lives together with common
laws, governments are necessary to enforce the aforementioned laws
and to show approval to citizens who act in an appropriate manner.
Like King Ahasuerus, who rewarded Mordecai for his good actions
(Esther 6:7-10), governments may make provisions to reward those
who abide by their laws. In rewarding socially acceptable behavior
and punishing behavior that is socially unacceptable, governments
implicitly affirm man's nature as a social being.

(3) God created the church to provide for man's social needs. This does not mean the church should be viewed as a social club or social organization. But it does mean that men reap social benefits by being members of the church for which Jesus died. If nothing more, clear benefits are associated with being around fellow Christians and assembling each week with them to worship God. And note the fact that edification – the action whereby one is built up by the words or deeds of another – stands as an important work of the church (Ephesians 4:16).

Conclusion

The claim that man is a social being is impossible to dispute. As 17th-century English poet John Donne wrote, "No man is an island entire of itself. Every man is a piece of the continent, a part of the main." [7] Our ability to communicate – along with the way we belong to families, live in communities, and worship together as congregations – stand as reminders about our social nature. And if those facts are not enough, we need only to be reminded that we were created in the very image of God (Genesis 1:27) – the One with whom we are to maintain fellowship (1 John 1:5-7). Clearly, man is a social being.

Questions for Consideration

1. What does Genesis 2:18 tell us about the nature of man?

2. Assess the statement made by Aristotle regarding man's ability to contribute to the well-being of other men. Do you think Aristotle is correct? Why or why not?

3. How does man's purpose play a role in understanding man as a social being?

4. In what way does fellowship serve to benefit your life?

5. How does the existence of the home prove that man is a social being?

6. How does the existence of the government support the claim that man is a social being?

7. What social benefits does one receive by being part of a congregation?

6

⚜

An Ethical Being

The Bible clearly asserts that man will be held accountable for his actions. The apostle Paul wrote, "For we must all appear before the judgment seat of Christ, that each one may receive the things done in the body, according to what he has done, whether good or bad" (2 Corinthians 5:10).

A careful examination of Paul's statement reveals two significant facts. (1) Man is responsible for what he does. This implies that one cannot seek to escape blame for his actions by arguing that his environment or genetic makeup diminish his capacity to act appropriately. (2) Man's actions will be judged as being either good or bad. This implies the existence of an objective standard. And if indeed an objective standard exists by which man is judged, then he possesses not only the ability but also the responsibility to act ethically. Thus, it is correct to describe man as an ethical being.

To say that man is an ethical being by nature is to say that man is endowed with certain characteristics that ensure his ability to act ethically. He has, for example, the ability to differentiate between what is morally right and wrong. As 18th-century Scottish philosopher Thomas Reid put it, "The subject of law must have the conception of a general

rule of conduct, which, without some degree of reason, he cannot have."
In addition, man is capable of framing his behavior on the foundation
of his knowledge of right and wrong. And if he, perchance, rejects the
right in favor of the wrong, he is culpable. This fact, Reid noted, serves
as "a sufficient inducement to obey the law, even when his strongest
animal desires draw him the contrary way." [1]

No matter what approach one advocates with regard to ethics, it is
generally admitted that the ability to behave ethically serves to distinguish
man from the rest of the physical world. In other words, as Kelly James
Clark and Anne Poortenga have written, "What makes us distinctively
human, what distinguishes us from the animals, is our ability to reason
and to rationally rule our desires." [2] This explains why "the ethical debates
from ancient through modern times have largely been over what makes
human beings essentially human and what sort of life enables that part of
our humanity to flourish." [3] In essence, humanity is inseparably linked
to ethical behavior. That does not mean mankind will always behave as
it should. As C.S. Lewis noted, "The law which is peculiar to [man's]
human nature, the law he does not share with animals or vegetables or
inorganic things, is the one he can disobey if he chooses." [4] Nevertheless,
men possess the capability of behaving properly.

The intention of this chapter is to build upon the idea that man is an
ethical being by describing and evaluating some of the major approaches
used as guidelines for ethical practice. Having done so, we will then
consider God's plan for man's behavior as well as one critical objection to that plan. Finally, we will seek to show that Scripture affirms
the idea that man is an ethical being and that his ethical behavior is
to mirror the behavior of the One in whose image man was created.

Approaches to Ethics

Generally speaking, ethical systems are classified into two divergent
categories. One category focuses primarily upon the end result and is
thus described as being *teleological* (end-centered). The other category,
based upon the duty that drives one to act, is classified as *deontological*
(duty-centered). One should not conclude that deontological approaches
to ethics are unconcerned with the final outcome, for that is not the
case. Nevertheless, a marked philosophical difference exists between

the two general categories of approaches to ethics. This passage from
Norman L. Geisler helps to explain:

> ... there is an important difference between the deontological
> use of results and a teleological use of them. In Christian eth-
> ics these results are all calculated within rules or norms. That
> is, no anticipated result as such can be used as a justification
> for breaking any God-given moral law. Utilitarians, on the
> other hand, use anticipated results to break moral rules. In
> fact, they use results to make the rules. Existing rules can
> be broken if the expected results call for it. For example,
> while Christian ethics allows for inoculation for disease, it
> does not allow for infanticide to purify the genetic stock of
> the human race; in this case the end result is used to justify
> the use of an evil means. In brief, the end may justify the
> use of good means, but it does not justify the use of any
> means, certainly not evil ones. [5]

While Geisler's quotation helps us to differentiate between the two
general categories of approaches to ethics, it also points to a potential
problem of all teleological systems: Those systems seemingly reject
the idea that absolute, objective moral laws exist. And if one grants that
no absolute behavioral norms exist, then he or she is left to speculate
and argue about how men ought to live. The problem with this is, of
course, that one cannot really argue effectively without a foundation
upon which to base that argument. As C.S. Lewis observed, "Quarrel-
ling means trying to show that the other man is in the wrong. And there
would be no sense in trying to do that unless you and he had some sort
of agreement as to what Right and Wrong are." [6] The issue becomes
whether ethical decisions can be tried or weighed against more than
personal preference. If not, then every man or woman becomes his or
her own authority; and if so, then every man or woman is amenable to
a higher law that governs his or her behavior. Before turning our attention to deontological systems, we will examine a few of the ethical
systems that could be classified as teleological.

   One of the most common approaches to ethics is known as *egoism*.
This approach derives behavior from the assumption that "the best

life is the one in which I succeed in getting what I want." [7] Thus, for the egoist, ethical behavior centers on his or her own situation. This does not mean a person practicing egoism always behaves selfishly; he or she may help someone else out of a sense of pity. What it does mean is that the egoist only considers his or her feelings in the matter. However, some glaring problems emerge from this approach – namely, egoism cannot provide an adequate answer as to why I should act in my own interests and not in the interest of others. Also, egoism cannot clearly distinguish between what one *wants* and what one *should want*. Paul wrote: "Let nothing be done through selfish ambition or conceit, but in lowliness of mind let each esteem others better than himself. Let each of you look out not only for his own interests, but also for the interests of others" (Philippians 2:3-4). In light of that warning, egoism clearly is not an adequate ethical approach.

Closely associated with egoism is the ethical approach known as **hedonism**. As explained by Louis Pojman, "The hedonist (derived from *hedon*, the Greek word for 'pleasure') asserts that all pleasure is good, that pleasure is the only thing good in itself, and that all other goodness is derived from this value." [8] Although hedonism appears to be a simple-minded approach, it is actually quite complex. The real problem lies in the fact that many actions cannot be said to be entirely pleasurable or entirely painful. Often a mixture of pleasure and pain is involved. For this reason, hedonists advocate actions that produce more pleasure than pain. In response, it should be noted that hedonism provides no reason to believe that pleasure equates to what is good. When Moses "refused to be called the son of Pharaoh's daughter, choosing rather to suffer affliction with the people of God than to enjoy the passing pleasures of sin" (Hebrews 11:24-25), he rejected hedonism in favor of doing God's will. And as King Solomon noted in Ecclesiastes 2:1, the life based solely upon pleasure is vanity.

A third teleological approach to ethics is known as **situationism**. Although its name seems to imply that it is nothing more than relativism, the approach – as advocated by its chief proponent, Joseph Fletcher – centers on the demands of love. As Norman L. Geisler has summarized,

The situationist holds that the general what and why are absolute, but the how is relative. There is an absolute prescription, but it is only worked out in the relative situation. Love is ultimate, but just how one is to love is dependant on the immediate circumstances. [9]

While this approach might sound appealing, it should be noted that we have no reason to think that love is the only absolute. Additionally, the theory assumes man is capable of always knowing what love demands. This, in itself, is debatable. Batsell Barrett Baxter therefore concluded:

Contrary to the view of the situationists, the Christian who believes the Bible to be the inspired Word of God believes that the rules and regulations which one finds in the Bible are framed by God for the express purpose of helping man to know what love requires in every situation of life. Rather than leaving the matter to man himself, so deeply and so emotionally involved in life, God lays down rules as to what loving behavior is in each situation. [10]

Utilitarianism is the final teleological approach we will consider in this chapter. This approach, generally associated with the writings of Jeremy Bentham (1748–1832) and John Stuart Mill (1806–1873), is set forth in a variety of ways. Generally, utilitarianism seeks the greatest good for the greatest number of people over time. One problem is that no adequate definition for the term "good" is offered. And with no solid basis, what is to keep one individual from doing what he supposes to be good and another individual from doing just the opposite with the same intentions in mind? Geisler correctly observes:

It begs the question to say that moral right is what brings the greatest good, for then we must ask what is 'good.' Either right and good are defined in terms of each other, which is circular reasoning, or good must be determined by some standard beyond the utilitarian process. [11]

Another problem is that utilitarianism cannot answer the question, as posed by Gordon Graham, "What reason do I have to promote the general happiness at the expense of my own personal happiness or the happiness of those nearest and dearest to me?" [12] Rather than thinking only of ourselves (as egoism does) or only of others (as utilitarianism asserts), the Bible challenges us to do both. Paul wrote, "See that no one renders evil for evil to anyone, but always pursue what is good both for yourselves and for all" (1 Thessalonians 5:15).

Dismissing the ethical approaches that focus upon the end result, it remains for us to consider ethical systems that concern themselves with the means or actions of individuals. One such system, Kantianism, is named for its proponent, 18th-century philosopher Immanuel Kant (1724–1804). Seeking to establish a rational approach to ethics that could be applied universally, Kant focused upon the concept of the "good will." This passage from Clark and Poortenga's *The Story of Ethics* explains:

> A good will is a will that acts from the motive of duty, that is, I do the right thing because it's the right thing; I do my duty simply because it's my duty. We might think of it this way: goodness does not depend on things going according to plan; rather, goodness depends on the plan itself. The good will believes it must follow the moral law even if all its inclinations and desired effects are thwarted. What makes a will good is not the actions it directs but *why* it directs those actions. [13]

But what determines the good in this system? Kant answered this by setting forth his Categorical Imperatives, the first two of which are (1) "Act only according to that maxim by which you can at the same time will that it should become a universal law" and (2) "Act so that you treat humanity, whether in your own person or in that of another, always as an end and never as a means only." [14] In evaluating Kant's plan, it does seem to prescribe how man ought to act. But the basis for this prescription – the Categorical Imperative – lacks objective support. As good as Kant's solution might sound, an opponent might correctly ask, what gives Kant the right to dictate how all men *ought* to live? An even more pressing problem is that Kant's approach to ethics fails to provide, as Thomas Reid put it, "a sufficient inducement to obey the law, even when his strongest animal desires draw him the contrary way." [15]

God's Plan for Man's Behavior

Setting aside the ethical approaches that focus upon the end and ignore the means as insufficient and rejecting Kant's approach to ethics because of its lack of motivation, we now turn our attention to an ethical plan that is *objective* (i.e., independent of man's ideas); *comprehensive* (i.e., concerned with both the end and the means); and *motivational* (i.e., providing sufficient reason for man to act appropriately). This plan, of course, is the one set forth in God's Word.

God's plan for man's behavior is objective in that it transcends man by springing from God: " 'For My thoughts are not your thoughts, Nor are your ways My ways,' says the LORD. 'For as the heavens are higher than the earth, So are My ways higher than your ways, And My thoughts than your thoughts' " (Isaiah 55:8-9). Likewise, God's plan is comprehensive in that it does not focus only on the end result or on the means required to get to the end. Instead, the plan addresses both how we live (the means) and where we will spend eternity (the end). A text that exemplifies both of these concerns is Titus 2:11-12, in which Paul wrote, "For the grace of God that brings salvation has appeared to all men, teaching us that, denying ungodliness and worldly lusts, we should live soberly, righteously, and godly in the present age."

Finally, God's plan provides sufficient motivation for man to obey – motivation that comes from the impending judgment day. On that day, "God will bring every work into judgment, Including every secret thing, Whether good or evil" (Ecclesiastes 12:14). And on that day, man will be judged by the very words of that plan (John 12:48).

A brief survey of Scripture will reveal the challenging nature of God's plan. God, for example, requires His followers to behave in a particular manner. Thus, Peter wrote, "but as He who called you is holy, you also be holy in all your conduct, because it is written, 'Be holy, for I am holy' " (1 Peter 1:15-16). God also expects His followers to deal respectfully and fairly with their fellow men. Jesus exhorted, "Therefore, whatever you want men to do to you, do also to them, for this is the Law and the Prophets" (Matthew 7:12) and "You shall love your neighbor as yourself" (22:39). Significantly, the plan of God places as much value on one individual's life as it does on a multitude (see Luke 15:3-10). For this reason, the individual who follows God is to consider the effects of his actions on both himself and others (1 Thessalonians 5:15). As an ethical being, man certainly has the capacity to do so.

The chief objection, raised by those who do not wish to acknowledge the authority of God's ethical plan, is that God's plan potentially collapses into arbitrariness. This conclusion is based upon the supposed *Euthyphro dilemma* set forth in Plato's *Euthyphro*. In that dialogue, Socrates asks Euthyphro the following question: "Is what is holy holy because the gods approve it, or do they approve it because it is holy?" [16] No matter how the question is answered, problems exist. Gordon Graham concludes, "What Plato's dialogue shows is that either good and bad are dependent upon the will of God, in which case they are a wholly arbitrary matter, or else they are not wholly arbitrary, in which case there is no room for any appeal to God." [17] Rather than answering that good is the result of God's decree or that God only decrees what is good, however, one might avoid the dilemma altogether by saying that good neither precedes or results from God, but rather flows from God. Just as God is love (1 John 4:8), God is also good. Thus, God's ethical plan for humanity is good because it comes from the very essence of God and is tied to His nature.

Conclusion

Certain expectations are associated with being created in God's image. One chief expectation is that we are to live differently than those creatures that were not created after the likeness of God. Man clearly has the ability not only to recognize the difference between what is good and evil, but also to do what is good and shun what is evil. When man acts in that manner, he acts ethically. But why should he do so? William K. Frankena observed, "The conditions of a satisfactory human life for people living in groups could hardly obtain otherwise." [18] But more important than man's social well-being is his spiritual status. Therefore, man should seek to live in a manner that brings glory and honor to his Maker. Jesus said, "Let your light so shine before men, that they may see your good works and glorify your Father in heaven" (Matthew 5:16).

Questions for Consideration

1. How can 2 Corinthians 5:10 be used to show that man is an ethical being?

2. What is the difference between the teleological and deontological approaches to ethics?

3. What is the main problem with all the teleological approaches to ethical behavior?

4. What does 1 Thessalonians 5:15 say about man's ethical approach?

5. How does God's ethical plan cover both the end and the means of one's behavior?

6. Why is it important for an ethical system to offer motivation for adherence?

7. What is the Euthyphro dilemma? How may the Christian respond to it?

8. How does being made in God's image relate to the idea that man is an ethical being?

7

A Privileged Being

Man occupies a unique position in the world – a fact accepted by both creationists and evolutionists. Although both groups maintain human beings are privileged, a vast difference exists between what the evolutionist means by "privileged" and what the creationist means. To the evolutionists, man is privileged simply because he is the most highly developed being. But to the one who believes in creation, the idea that man is privileged means much more.

The one who advocates evolution, the humanist, must praise man guardedly. He must recognize the precarious position of man. The following quotation from the book *Humanism Versus Theism* illustrates this point:

> Humanism quite willingly admits that man has wider relations which should be studied. He is a part of the universe, and it is impossible to determine the nature of the part until we know something about the character of the whole. Any attempt to determine those relations in the widest possible sense humanism welcomes. Through the study of our wider environment we may be forced to change our present opinion concerning ourselves. [1]

That last statement – "we may be forced to change our present opinion concerning ourselves" – reveals a depth of uncertainty that permeates those who reject God's existence. Although the evolutionist or humanist would like to affirm that man is privileged in an unqualified sense, he cannot do so and be consistent. He must allow for future variations or discoveries. As far as he is concerned, man is perched atop the evolutionary chain for now. Nevertheless, the evolutionist must leave room for further developments.

In stark contrast, the creationist can argue that man is privileged in an unqualified manner. This is true, first and foremost, because man was created in the very image of God (Genesis 1:27). And because man is spiritual as well as physical, he has been placed in a position of authority over the physical creation (vv. 28-29). Describing this great blessing God bestowed upon man, the psalmist wrote: "You have crowned him with glory and honor. You have made him to have dominion over the works of Your hands; You have put all things under his feet" (Psalm 8:5-6). Clearly, Scripture affirms that man is privileged. But in what ways is this true?

Man Is Privileged Physically

The physical prowess of man cannot always be credited to his superior strength or speed; certainly, many animals are much stronger and faster. Thus, when we argue that man is privileged in a physical sense, we are saying his physical position of authority is due as much, if not more so, to his brain as to his brawn. God's command to "fill the earth and subdue it" (Genesis 1:28) was based on His understanding of man's complete being. In other words, God knew man possessed both the physical ability and the mental acumen to accomplish the task. Man, then, is physically privileged because of his ability to learn, remember and adjust to his circumstances.

In no area is man's privileged physical position seen more clearly than in his ability to deal with and respond to pain. While we might not initially grasp the importance of the ability to feel pain, man's capacity to react and respond to pain is critical to his well-being. That is not to say that animals lack the ability to feel pain. Harold S. Kushner wrote: "Animals feel that sort of pain even as we do. You don't need to have a soul to feel pain when something sharp is stuck into your flesh. There is another level of pain, however, which only human beings can feel.

Only human beings can find meaning in their pain." As Kushner seems
to indicate, man can use pain as a sort of steppingstone:

> We may not ever understand why we suffer or be able to
> control the forces that cause our suffering, but we can have a
> lot to say about what the suffering does to us, and what sort of
> people we become because of it. Pain makes some people bitter
> and envious. It makes others sensitive and compassionate. It
> is the result, not the cause, of pain that makes some experi-
> ences of pain meaningful and others empty and destructive. [2]

It would be accurate to say that man's privileged physical position
stems, at least in part, from his ability to control his emotions. But it
would be just as accurate to say that man's physical superiority is based
upon his ability to remember. One's memory not only provides a frame
of reference for future decisions, but also a web of support. That is not
to say memories are always pleasant, for they are not. But just as man
has the ability to react to his pain in the appropriate manner, he also
has the ability to respond appropriately to previous events.

Scripture often charges us to do this very thing. For instance,
1 Corinthians 10:11-12 states: "Now all these things happened to
them as examples, and they were written for our admonition, upon
whom the ends of the ages have come. Therefore let him who thinks
he stands take heed lest he fall." In that text, Paul cited the behavior of
the Israelites as an example for Christians to avoid, and he cautioned
man not only to look backward, but also to reflect upon his own position. This implies that man's ability to remember previous events and
learn from the mistakes and successes of history helps him to succeed.
Animals lack this ability. Thus, man is a physically privileged being.

Man Is Privileged Spiritually

As privileged as man is physically, that privilege pales in comparison
to the spiritual position he enjoys. Among the spiritual benefits available to man are the ability to become a child of God, the opportunity
to live as a brother to mankind, and the ability to experience the blessings of forgiveness and salvation. No wonder Paul wrote, "If in this
life only we have hope in Christ, we are of all men the most pitiable"

(1 Corinthians 15:19). As great as man's physical life can be, especially when he develops a relationship with Christ, that life is pitiable when compared with the spiritual.

Man can become a child of God. One of the greatest spiritual blessings – and one that certainly demonstrates how privileged man can be – is the blessing of being a child of God. Describing this, the apostle John wrote, "Behold what manner of love the Father has bestowed on us, that we should be called children of God!" (1 John 3:1). Because of God's love, Jesus was sent to die upon the cross (John 3:16). And that same unceasing love makes it possible for man to become God's child. Guy N. Woods commented:

> "Manner of love" is a phrase descriptive of the quality of love which the Father has vouchsafed to his children. In it is revealed not only the size, but the blessedness of it. "What glorious, sublime, immeasurable love the Father has bestowed upon us ... ." Included in the manner of it is the freeness, the greatness, the preciousness, the scope, the duration – in a word, all that is summed up in the word, "For God so loved the world, that he gave his only begotten Son ..." (John 3:16). This love God "bestowed" (literally, gave), eventuating in our being "called children of God." Inasmuch as the Lord makes us what we are, to be called his children by him is to be such, and to sustain this relation to him in all the affairs of life. [3]

But how does being God's child make man spiritually privileged? It does so by providing man with benefits reserved only for God's children. Among these benefits is the opportunity to receive an eternal inheritance. Paul noted that "if [we are] children [of God], then [we are] heirs – heirs of God and joint heirs with Christ, if indeed we suffer with Him, that we may also be glorified together" (Romans 8:17). In addition, those who are God's children have access to the throne of God by means of prayer. Jesus made this clear with His statement in Matthew 7:11: "If you then, being evil, know how to give good gifts to your children, how much more will your Father who is in heaven give good things to those who ask Him!" God has made the avenue of prayer available to man, but it will only avail those who enjoy the proper relationship with Him: His children (see James 5:16; 1 Peter 3:12).

So how does man become a child of God? According to Paul in Galatians 3:26-27, man does so through faithful obedience: "For you are all sons of God through faith in Christ Jesus. For as many of you as were baptized into Christ have put on Christ." Significantly, the same action that enables one to enjoy the privileged spiritual position of sonship with God – faithful obedience culminating in baptism – also puts one "in Christ." And because all spiritual blessings are located in Christ (Ephesians 1:3) – including no condemnation (Romans 8:1), redemption (Ephesians 1:7), an inheritance (v. 11), grace (2 Timothy 2:1) and salvation (v. 10) – it naturally follows that those who desire to be blessed spiritually must be obedient to God's plan.

Man can have spiritual brethren. The privileges associated with spiritual brotherhood stem from the support Christians offer to one another. Those who have faced great difficulties have the ability to comfort individuals who experience similar trials (2 Corinthians 1:3-4), and those who buckle under the burden of sin can be helped along by those who are strong (Galatians 6:1-2). Rather than thinking only of ourselves, we are to consider the difficulties of others (Philippians 2:4). When our brethren rejoice, we are to rejoice; when our brethren weep, we are to weep (Romans 12:15). We may be encouraged by the successes of those who have gone before us (Hebrews 12:1), and we may rest easier knowing God's plan for the church makes provisions for men to watch out for the souls of their brethren (13:17). Man is spiritually privileged when he has brothers and sisters in Christ who care for his well-being.

Man can experience the blessings of forgiveness and salvation. Another wonderful spiritual privilege is the opportunity to be forgiven of sin and to enjoy the eternal bliss of heaven. Because man's sins separate him from God (Isaiah 59:1-2) and because "the wages of sin is death" (Romans 6:23), clearly a plan to redeem mankind was necessary. This plan could not be based on man's possessions, for "without shedding of blood there is no remission" (Hebrews 9:22). Thus, as Jesus noted, "it was necessary for the Christ to suffer and to rise from the dead the third day, and that repentance and remission of sins should be preached in His name to all nations, beginning at Jerusalem" (Luke 24:46-47). In His death, Jesus shed the blood that washes man's sins away (Revelation 1:5), and in man's obedience, he contacts that cleansing blood (Acts 22:16). David Lipscomb correctly observed, "Obedience to the truth brings us to the blood that cleanses, and so we are said to be cleansed by that which brings us to the cleansing power." [4] Man, then, is spiritually privileged in that he may benefit from the plan of God that sent the Son of God to pay the ransom for the sins of humanity.

When man obeys Jesus, he submits to the "author of eternal salvation" (Hebrews 5:9). This submission enables man to long for the eternal home in heaven. Heaven is the place Jesus promised to prepare (John 14:1-4), and in heaven there will be no pain or sorrow or difficulty (Revelation 21:4). As Paul noted, the hope of heaven is what enables us to face the difficulties of life (Romans 8:18). If all other means of convincing man of his privilege were to fail, the description of God's plan, Jesus' death, and the "inheritance incorruptible and undefiled and that does not fade away, reserved in heaven" (1 Peter 1:4) would serve to establish that man is a privileged being.

Conclusion

As he considered the way God deals with mankind, the psalmist wrote, "Bless the LORD, O my soul, And forget not all His benefits" (Psalm 103:2). The benefits God has provided to mankind certainly are worth remembering. This is especially true when one realizes those benefits have set man apart, physically and spiritually, from the rest of the creation. Brad Harrub and Bert Thompson correctly observed:

> The Bible paints a picture of man as a being that stands on a different level from all other creatures upon the Earth. He towers high above all earthly creation because of the phenomenal powers and attributes that God Almighty has freely given him. No other living being was given the capacities and capabilities, the potential and the dignity, that God instilled in each man and woman. Humankind is the peak, the pinnacle, the crown, the apex of God's creation. And what a difference it should make in our lives. [5]

Truly, man is a privileged being!

Questions for Consideration

1. How do evolutionists and creationists differ in their descriptions of man as a privileged being?

2. How does man's ability to deal with pain show that he is physically privileged?

3. In what other ways could one describe man as physically privileged?

4. How does one become a child of God?

5. In what way(s) does man's ability to live as a spiritual brother help to distinguish him as a privileged being?

6. What does God's plan for man's salvation say about how God views mankind?

7. How does the concept of heaven serve to bolster the idea that man is a privileged being?

8

A Sexual Being

After He created man, God provided the following instructions: "Be fruitful and multiply; fill the earth and subdue it" (Genesis 1:28). Implicit within this statement is the idea that man has the ability to reproduce after his own kind. This ability, as the statement also implies, is a necessary and inseparable aspect of man's being. Thus, it is appropriate to say man is a sexual being. That is not to say that the discussion of human sexuality is concerned only with one's ability to engage in a reproductive act. As we will notice, Scripture spends much more time focusing on the appropriate place and function of sexual behavior than it does the fact of it. Numerous warnings also are issued regarding the misuse of the sexual relationship.

The importance of understanding this subject is obvious when one considers that man's sexual behavior not only affects him physically but also spiritually. In making this point, the apostle Paul warned: "Flee sexual immorality. Every sin that a man does is outside the body, but he who commits sexual immorality sins against his own body" (1 Corinthians 6:18). Paul's assertion does not mean sexuality is wrong in the proper context. Bill Flatt has correctly observed:

God created sexuality, and it is good (Gen. 1:26-29). We
may misuse it, but sexuality in itself is not evil. God intended for people to be heterosexual and not homosexual.
He made them male and female and told them to multiply
(Gen. 1:26-28). Every sexual act in the Bible that is endorsed
is heterosexual sex in marriage (Lev. 18, 20; 1 Cor. 6:9-11;
Rom. 1:18-28; 1 Cor. 7:1-5; Heb. 13:4). Married couples are
encouraged to be ecstatic with one another (Prov. 5:18-19).
God created sex to be enjoyed in marriage, to bring people
together, and to reproduce people. [1]

Regrettably, our world seems to have lost its way when it comes
to understanding man's sexual nature. Perhaps this is because of the
sexual propaganda that surrounds us daily, or perhaps it is because
behavior once viewed as shameful is now flaunted. But most likely it
is because God's plan for man's sexual behavior has been cast aside.
Like the psalmist, we may ask, "If the foundations are destroyed, What
can the righteous do?" (Psalm 11:3). The only correct response is to
turn our attention back to God's Word. So what does Scripture say
about man's sexual behavior?

The Purposes of the Sexual Relationship

Although many glorify sex as an activity that exists for its own sake,
Scripture certainly does not describe it that way. In fact, Scripture not
only limits sexual behavior to within the lawful marriage relationship,
but it also designates three purposes of sexual behavior. (1) The most
obvious purpose of sex is procreation. As has already been noted, God
commanded man to "be fruitful and multiply" (Genesis 1:28). Augustine
of Hippo (A.D. 354–430), in his treatise "On the Good of Marriage,"
expounded upon this point:

God gives us some goods that are to be sought for their own
sake, such as wisdom, health, friendship: but others, which
are necessary for the sake of somewhat, such as learning,
meat, drink, sleep, marriage, sexual intercourse. For of these
certain are necessary for the sake of wisdom, as learning:
certain for the sake of health, as meat and drink and sleep:

certain for the sake of friendship, as marriage or sexual intercourse: for hence subsists the propagation of the human kind, wherein friendly fellowship is a great good. [2]

Regardless of whether one agrees with Augustine's list of goods that should be sought for their own sake, it must be admitted that man's sexual ability exists, at least in part, for the reproduction of other humans. But to say sexual activity exists only for one purpose is to argue for less than what Scripture allows.

(2) Another purpose for sex, inherently present within the concept of the "one flesh" relationship (Genesis 2:24), is the development of intimacy between spouses. Robert P. George has described this:

Again, the intrinsic point of sex in any marriage, fertile or not, is, in our view, the basic good of the marriage itself, considered as a two-in-one-flesh communion of persons that is consummated and actualized by acts of the reproductive type. Such acts alone among sexual acts can be truly unitive, and thus marital; and marital acts, thus understood, have their intelligibility and value intrinsically, and not merely by virtue of their capacity to facilitate the realization of other goods. [3]

In other words, the sexual relationship that exists between husband and wife is not a selfish relationship. It is instead a very special blessing that helps facilitate the greater pleasure of developing and strengthening the marriage bond.

This idea seems to be what Paul sought to promote in his first letter to the Corinthians. After warning the Corinthians to avoid fornication, which would thus violate the "one flesh" relationship reserved for marriage (1 Corinthians 6:16), Paul went on to provide divine instructions designed to govern the sexual relationship between husband and wife:

Let the husband render to his wife the affection due her, and likewise also the wife to her husband. The wife does not have authority over her own body, but the husband does. And likewise the husband does not have authority over his own body, but the wife does. Do not deprive one another except with consent for a time, that you may give yourselves to fasting and prayer; and come together again so that Satan does not tempt you because of your lack of self-control (1 Corinthians 7:3-5).

These instructions were not written to lessen the romantic nature of the sexual relationship. Instead, they were given with the intention of helping both men and women to avoid falling victim to sexual temptations (1 Corinthians 7:2), which brings us to the final reason for sexual activity.

(3) Sex helps to prevent men and women from sinning sexually. When one realizes that God's purpose for creating the institution of marriage was to fill a void that otherwise would have been present (Genesis 2:18), the roles intended for both husband and wife come into focus. Describing these roles, H. Leo Boles noted:

> Marriage is an institution ordained by God for the honor and happiness of mankind, in which one man and one woman enter into a bodily and spiritual union, pledging each to the other's mutual love, honor, fidelity, sympathy, forbearance, and comradeship, such as should assure an unbroken continuance of their wedlock so long as both shall live. [4]

Clearly, the sexual relationship (or "bodily union," as Boles put it) plays a role in helping the marriage relationship develop into what God intended. When husbands and wives realize the beauty and blessings associated with becoming "one flesh" (Genesis 2:24), they will appreciate more fully why Paul instructed husbands to "love their own wives as their own bodies" (Ephesians 5:28). Viewed in light of the purposes assigned to it by God, the sexual relationship is revealed to be beautiful and wholesome.

The Place of the Sexual Relationship

Locating the sexual relationship within the bonds of matrimony, the author of Hebrews wrote, "Marriage is honorable among all, and the bed undefiled; but fornicators and adulterers God will judge" (13:4). According to one commentary, this text "suggests that the union is defiled if marriage is not respected as the only context for sexual relations." [5] In essence, we can conclude that within the context of marriage, sex is not only acceptable but both beautiful and beneficial; outside of the marriage relationship, however, sex is shameful and draws the judgment of God. Daniel Akin has correctly observed:

> God knows nothing about casual sex, because in reality there is no such thing. What is often called casual sex is always costly. Sexually transmitted disease (STDs), unexpected pregnancy, and psychological and spiritual scars are some of the results, and the price paid, because we have approached God's good gift of sex all too casually. Sexual attraction is inevitable. It is what God intended. However, unless we follow God's plan, we will miss out on His best and suffer the painful and tragic consequences in the process. [6]

As in all other cases, God's way – the only way – is clearly the best! What, then, does God intend for the married couple's sexual relationship to be like? We find at least two things. (1) He intends for this relationship to be one of exclusivity and fulfillment. Solomon charged his son:

> Drink water from your own cistern, And running water from your own well. Should your fountains be dispersed abroad, Streams of water in the streets? Let them be only your own, And not for strangers with you. Let your fountain be blessed, And rejoice with the wife of your youth. As a loving deer and a graceful doe, Let her breasts satisfy you at all times; And always be enraptured with her love. For why should you, my son, be enraptured by an immoral woman, And be embraced in the arms of a seductress? (Proverbs 5:15-20)

Ted Burleson has noted, "Husbands are to find the satisfaction and joy in their wives that they could not find in a seductress on the street (Proverbs 5:15; Ecclesiastes 9:9)." [7]

(2) God intends the sexual relationship to be an avenue through which husbands and wives express the love they have for one another. Burleson continued: "When a husband and wife have sexual intercourse it is not sex. It is lovemaking. God gave sex as an expression of love between husband and wife (Song of Solomon 1:12-15; 3:1-5)." [8] As suggested, this "expression of love" is perhaps best described in the Song of Solomon.

Describing the passionate relationship that existed between Solomon and his beloved, the Song of Songs, as the book is also called, paints a picture of romantic love. One author summarized the contents of the book and the blessing it can be to those who learn from it:

> The Song of Songs explains the purpose and place of sex as God designed it. When we make love the way God planned, we enjoy the security of a committed relationship, experience the joy of unreserved passion, and discover the courage to give ourselves completely to another in unhindered abandonment. [9]

The following chart lists several of the lessons from Song of Solomon that married couples would do well to consider:

To Sing Solomon's Song ...

- Spouses should desire one another (Song of Solomon 1:2-4).
- Spouses should compliment one another (1:15-17; 4:1-11).
- Each spouse should feel like his or her spouse stands out in a crowd (2:2-3).
- Spouses should dream or think about one another when they are not together (2:10-14).
- Spouses should feel a sense of ownership over one another (6:3).
- Spouses should make plans to be together and set aside time to be intimate (7:11-13).
- Spouses should have a love for one another that will never be quenched (8:6-7).

Perversions of the Sexual Relationship

Although it is clear that God has defined the boundaries for authorized sexual behavior, it is just as clear that man has often ignored those boundaries. Consequently, marriages are torn apart by fornication, lives are forever scarred by rape or incest, homosexual behavior is paraded and even encouraged in some circles, and the consumption of pornography has risen to epidemic proportions. But why are all these deviant sexual behaviors so common?

To answer this question, it should first be noted that mankind often has failed to grasp or respect the purposes of man's sexual capacity. Rather than considering that sexual activity plays a role in facilitating greater goods – such as procreation, intimacy in marriage, and as a help to overcoming temptation – sex (or more specifically, the pleasure that results from it) is viewed as the ultimate good. Not surprisingly, this approach naturally leads those who advocate it to cast aside moral restraints in pursuit of more pleasure and pleasure of a more intense kind. What they fail to realize is that man's sexual nature, like his ethical nature, must be based upon much more than what one wants at the moment. Like Esau, who sold his birthright for a bowl of stew, those who commit fornication give away a precious commodity (e.g., virginity) for a passing pleasure (Hebrews 12:16-17). But as we noted in our response to hedonism in an earlier chapter, we have no reason to conclude that *pleasure* is parallel to *good*, and we have every reason to shun the temporary allurements of the world in favor of the eternal reward awaiting those who obey God (1 John 2:15-17).

The second and perhaps most obvious reason sexual perversion abounds is that many individuals have completely disregarded God's plan. That plan was clearly enunciated by Jesus in Matthew 19:4-6:

> Have you not read that He who made them at the beginning "made them male and female," and said, "For this reason a man shall leave his father and mother and be joined to his wife, and the two shall become one flesh"? So then, they are no longer two but one flesh. Therefore what God has joined together, let not man separate.

At least four important facts are found in this short statement. (1) The sexual relationship is to occur between partners of the opposite sex. God created man to be with woman and woman to be with man. Because a simple look at the anatomy of men and women reveals this fact, any other relationship is both unnatural and shameful (Romans 1:26-27). (2) The sexual relationship is to be exclusive and unitive. The man and woman who engage in a sexual relationship are to rely upon each other and use that relationship as a means to grow closer together. (3) The sexual relationship exists for the benefit of both spouses. Because "they are no longer two but one flesh" (Matthew 19:6), selfishness has no place in the marriage relationship. Thus, Paul wrote: "The wife does not have authority over her own body, but the husband does. And likewise the husband does not have authority over his own body, but the wife does" (1 Corinthians 7:4). (4) Those who engage in the "one flesh" relationship are to be married – joined together by God – and not to be separated by man. The exception to this rule, given by Jesus in the same context, is in the case of fornication (Matthew 19:9).

Respect for these godly principles would cause the sexual perversions so common in our society to cease. If individuals would recognize that the sexual relationship is intended for members of the opposite sex, homosexual behavior would end. Norman L. Geisler's comments on this point are worth noting:

> God ordained that sex should be used within the context of a monogamous heterosexual relationship. Homosexual practices are contrary to God's ordained pattern for human beings. In addition, the Bible speaks out explicitly and forcefully against homosexual practices. The Old Testament considered it a capital offense, and the New Testament treats it as grounds for excommunication. Indeed, Paul declared that no homosexual would inherit the kingdom of God. The language of Scripture could scarcely be more emphatic. Homosexual practices are called unnatural, impure, shameful, indecent, perverse, and an abomination. [10]

If individuals would recognize the exclusivity and unity God intends for the sexual relationship, perversions such as rape, incest, and the use of pornography would cease. If individuals would recognize that the sexual relationship exists for the benefit of both spouses and if each would seek to meet the various needs of the spouse, adulterous behavior would occur less frequently. If individuals would recognize that marriage involves not only a husband and wife but also God, divorce would not be so prevalent. Adherence to God's plan would eradicate sexual perversion.

Conclusion

Man's sexual nature should not be taken lightly. The sexual relationship is truly a gift from God to be cherished and enjoyed. At the same time, man must be extremely careful not to misuse it. No wonder Paul admonished: "Flee sexual immorality. Every sin that a man does is outside the body, but he who commits sexual immorality sins against his own body" (1 Corinthians 6:18). Certain dangers are associated with sexual sins that eclipse the dangers associated with many other actions. As one commentator has written, "Other sins may be harmful to the body, but this one is more. In fornication people lower themselves, shed their dignity and honor, become completely carnal and corrupt." [11] Let us realize the challenges man faces as a sexual being, and let us strive to understand and honor the purposes and place that God has assigned to human sexuality.

Questions for Consideration

1. Why is it important to understand that man is a sexual being?

2. What are the three purposes of the sexual relationship described in the chapter?

3. Why is the concept of "one flesh" significant?

4. What is the meaning of Proverbs 5:15-20?

5. How would a careful study of Song of Solomon help husbands and wives to improve their sexual relationships?

6. What four principles regarding sexual behavior are found in Matthew 19:4-6?

7. How would respecting these four principles help to eradicate various sexual perversions?

9

A Freewill Being

As he stood before the Roman governor Felix, the apostle Paul made his case for Christianity and "reasoned about righteousness, self-control, and the judgment to come" (Acts 24:25). Significantly, all three components of his message – righteousness, self-control and judgment – rely upon the concept that man has the capability, at least in some way, to control his actions. If man lacks the ability to live righteously, why stress righteousness? If man is not free to control his own actions, why mention self-control? And if man is nothing more than an automaton, why speak about the coming judgment? The implication of Paul's appeal to these concepts is that man is a freewill being.

But what does it mean to say that man possesses free will? How does this concept fit with God's sovereignty? And in what way does God's foreknowledge affect man's freedom? Any adequate discussion about this subject must address these and similar questions, which is what we intend to do in this chapter. Above all, however, the idea that man has the ability to make meaningful decisions – an ability that serves to define him – will be defended.

The Assertion of Freedom

Even a cursory glance at Scripture will uncover several passages asserting man's free will. It is implicitly established near the beginning of Genesis when God instructed Adam and Eve to refrain from eating fruit from the tree of the knowledge of good and evil (Genesis 2:17; 3:2-3). Despite this warning, they willfully yielded to their own desires and sinned: "So when the woman saw that the tree was good for food, that it was pleasant to the eyes, and a tree desirable to make one wise, she took of its fruit and ate. She also gave to her husband with her, and he ate" (3:6). As a result, God punished Adam and Eve and removed them from the garden (vv. 22-24). Adam and Eve could not blame their sin on their parents, for they had none. Likewise, they could not blame their sin on their environment, for it was the best man has ever known. Neither could they blame God, for He had warned them not to eat the forbidden fruit. So why did Adam and Eve sin? The only explanation is because of their own free will.

From that point in Scripture onward, we find numerous passages that ascribe freedom of choice to mankind. Moses explicitly challenged the Israelites: "I call heaven and earth as witnesses today against you, that I have set before you life and death, blessing and cursing; therefore choose life, that both you and your descendants may live" (Deuteronomy 30:19). Perhaps more famous is the statement found in Joshua's farewell address: "Choose for yourselves this day whom you will serve" (Joshua 24:15). Consider the assertion of Jesus: "If anyone wills to do His will, he shall know concerning the doctrine, whether it is from God or whether I speak on My own authority" (John 7:17). And note the invitation recorded in Revelation 22:17: "And the Spirit and the bride say, 'Come!' And let him who hears say, 'Come!' And let him who thirsts come. Whoever desires, let him take the water of life freely." Clearly, man's ability to make significant choices is set forth in Scripture. With this in mind, it is not surprising to read that Moses "refused to be called the son of Pharaoh's daughter, choosing rather to suffer affliction with the people of God than to enjoy the passing pleasures of sin" (Hebrews 11:24-25).

If man is not free to choose his own actions, then the concept of personal accountability seems to lose meaning. Arguing this point, Kerry Duke has written:

One of the clearest indications of free will is the Bible's emphasis on personal accountability to God. This theme plays a central role in the overall message of the Bible. Man has always tried to escape this truth by placing the blame for his sins on someone or something else. But the Bible lays the blame where it belongs – at the feet of the person who committed the act. The Bible teaches that each person is responsible for his own actions. ... God does not allow us to be tempted beyond our ability to withstand temptation (I Cor. 10:13). As a result, "each one of us shall give an account of himself to God" (Rom. 14:12). Each person will be judged according to his works (Rev. 20:12; II Cor. 5:10). In a day when men refuse to take responsibility for their actions, the Bible offers a refreshing perspective. [1]

If God can hold man accountable for his actions, then it certainly seems man is free to choose how he lives. This is the picture we find painted in Scripture.

The Meaning of Freedom

Just because we may conclude that the Bible describes man as being free, we should not conclude that everyone who believes the Bible understands freedom to mean the same thing. In reality, two divergent views are commonly held by those who recognize human freedom. One view is that freedom simply means man has the right to do as he chooses or desires. This view of freedom, known as *compatibilism*, asserts that a person can be free even if he only has one option. To illustrate this view, consider this scenario:

Suppose that a man is brought into a room while asleep. The door, which is the only way out of the room, is then securely bolted from the outside. The man does not know that the door is bolted, does not know, therefore, that he *cannot* leave the room. He awakens, finds himself in the room, looks around and notices that there are friendly people in the room with whom he would like to converse. Accordingly, he stays in the room rather than leave. [2]

This approach to human freedom appeals to those who adhere to the tenets promoted by John Calvin (1509–1564). One of those tenets – the doctrine of predestination – holds that men "are not all created with a similar destiny; but eternal life is foreordained for some, and eternal damnation for others. Every man ... is predestinated either to life or to death." The compatibilist view of freedom fits Calvin's theology in that it helps absolve God from any guilt with regard to man's sin: The choice of man to sin is a free one, even though God provided him no other alternative. In essence, "Man, therefore, falls according to the *appointment* of Divine Providence, but he falls by his own fault." [3]

But is man really free if only one choice is possible? The following objection by Manuel Velasquez seems reasonable:

> If we are not free to act against our desires, then isn't there still a clear sense in which we are not free? Maybe we are "free" in the sense that we are not chained down and physically restrained from acting. But aren't we unfree in the more important sense that we do not ultimately control what we do? [4]

This leads us to consider the alternate view of freedom: *incompatibilism*. The incompatibilist view of freedom, also known as libertarianism, is that a person is free only if he or she has the ability to engage or not engage in an action. In essence, the individual is in complete control of his actions. Jesus' statement in John 10:18, in which He described His life, seems to have special relevance to this subject: "No one takes it from Me, but I lay it down of Myself. I have power to lay it down, and I have power to take it again. This command I have received from My Father." Regardless of whatever else one might say, Jesus certainly seemed to be saying that He had the ability to choose either to die or to refrain from dying. As author D.A. Carson has explained, "Jesus went to the cross voluntarily: he *chose* to obey the Father. He prayed, 'Not my will, but yours be done!' – a prayer that needed praying, even though at one level it is scarcely conceivable that God's redemptive will on the cross could not have been accomplished." [5] Nevertheless, if this is an accurate interpretation, then Jesus experienced freedom in the fullest sense of the term.

Philosophical Challenges
to Man's Freedom

If one accepts that man is free in the fullest sense of the word –
free either to act or *not* act – then certain questions arise that must
be answered. Chiefly, how is it possible to reconcile man's freedom
with God's sovereignty? Those adhering to the compatibilist view of
freedom – namely, Calvinists – do not view this as a serious problem.
Asserting God's complete sovereignty, the Calvinist holds that "God
knows what will take place in the future because he has decreed what
will take place, and nothing can thwart his intentions." [6] At the same
time, the Calvinist also affirms that man remains free in the sense that
he always chooses to do what God has decreed.

But does this approach really resolve the issue? Do we have valid
reasons to believe that the compatibilist view of freedom is an accurate
understanding of that term? This critique by William J. Abraham hints
that we do not:

> The objection to Calvin's position based on this analysis is
> obvious. The reprobate do what they want; they sin and rebel
> to their hearts' content. They cannot, however, do otherwise.
> Given the desires, beliefs, wants, and so forth, that God has
> allotted them by his providence, they must act as they do.
> Hence they are not free or morally culpable for their actions.
> When they appear before God and are held accountable for
> not being honest, loving, patient, they can honestly say that
> they could not do otherwise. Given the way that God controls
> the inner operations of their lives, they had to act as they did. [7]

Rather than striking a balance between God's sovereignty and man's
freedom, Calvinism's approach seems to pick one side (God) over the
other (man's freedom).

But what is the alternative? How can individuals who believe man is
truly free reconcile divine sovereignty with human freedom? There are
three things we must remember. (1) It was the sovereign God who chose
to create man. (2) The Godhead upholds all things (Hebrews 1:3) and
in God "we live and move and have our being" (Acts 17:28). (3) As an
omniscient being, God knows all things (i.e., He is capable of "declaring

the end from the beginning, And from ancient times things that are not yet done" [Isaiah 46:10]). With this in mind, however, we must stress that saying God *knows* all things is not the same as saying God *causes* all things. William L. Rowe has written:

> He knows in advance the events that will take place by *foreseeing* them, not by *foreordaining* them. The doctrine of divine foreknowledge, then, does not presuppose the doctrine of divine predestination. ... There does not appear to be any conflict between divine foreknowledge and human freedom. For although God's *foreordaining* something makes that something happen, his *foreknowing* does not make it happen. Things occur not because God foreknows them; rather, he foreknows them because they occur. [8]

As Kerry Duke has explained, "God's knowledge of 'future' acts does not cause those acts any more than His knowledge of past acts causes them. Our problem is that we try to analyze this problem through limited human vision." [9] Duke's final comment may well be the key. Instead of looking at God's foreknowledge from man's time-bound perspective, it may be more appropriate to say God views things as if removed from time. Rather than seeing things as being past, present or future, God simply sees things as they are.

Even if we have shown that God's foreknowledge and man's freedom are compatible, one final step remains in the process of reconciling divine sovereignty and human freedom. This step relies on the idea that God has created and placed man at the perfect *epistemic distance*. Explaining this concept, Thomas B. Warren wrote:

> Proper "epistemic distance" means that man must not be so *close* (epistemically – i.e., "distance" related to *knowledge*) to God that he is so *overwhelmed* by the immediate presence of Deity (or by the *evidence* for him) that it is *impossible* for him to *avoid* believing in God, and that he must not be so *far away* (epistemically) from God that he cannot be *drawn* to God by the evidence provided for him in that environment. [10]

Scripture affirms that God has placed man at the appropriate epistemic distance to make free moral agency possible. Although He has "allowed all nations to walk in their own ways," He also has provided ample evidence for individuals to know of His existence (Acts 14:16-17). While we, in seeking the Lord, "might grope for Him and find Him," the reality is that "He is not far from each one of us" (17:27). God is near enough so we can know Him if we desire, but He is far enough removed from us so we are not overwhelmed by Him, thus losing our capacity to act freely. Herein lies the explanation for the delicate balance that exists between God's sovereignty and man's freedom.

The Result of Freedom

Having shown that the Bible asserts man is free and having defined freedom and defended the concept against a prominent challenge, it remains for us to consider the *result* of man's freedom. Obviously, one thing that results from freedom is sin. When we consider that true freedom means a person can either act upon his desires or counter them, it becomes obvious that sin – which is rooted in selfishness – is possible. Adam and Eve sinned and lost their place in Eden (Genesis 3:23-24), and some of the angels also sinned and were cast from God's presence (2 Peter 2:4).

Because sin is a transgression of God's law (1 John 3:4), then the one who sins rebels against God. Such rebellion results in separation (Isaiah 59:1-2) and is rightly viewed as an affront to God. When man sins, he chooses his own desires over the desires of God. And the very idea that man can choose to turn his back on God helps us understand why sin is so despicable. As psychiatrist Karl Menninger put it,

> The wrongness of the sinful act lies not merely in its non-conformity, its departure from the accepted, appropriate way of behavior, but in an implicit aggressive quality – a ruthlessness, a hurting, a breaking away from God and from the rest of humanity, a partial alienation, or act of rebellion. [11]

Nevertheless, if man is truly free, he must be free either to accept God or to reject Him. Sin is a direct result of man's freedom.

A second result of freedom, and a consequence of sin, is suffering. That is not to say that all suffering results from the free decisions of men; some suffering occurs simply because of the type of world in which we live. But just as surely, other instances of suffering take place because of the free choices of men. D.A. Carson observed, "Evil is the primal cause of suffering, rebellion is the root of pain, sin is the source of death." [12] And Solomon wrote, "Good understanding gains favor, But the way of the unfaithful is hard" (Proverbs 13:15).

Lest we become discouraged and think freedom only facilitates pain and suffering, we must be reminded about two wonderful promises in Scripture. (1) Although we face great trials in this life, they will end in reward for those who freely choose to serve God. Paul wrote, "For I consider that the sufferings of this present time are not worthy to be compared with the glory which shall be revealed in us" (Romans 8:18). (2) The reward will be worth the wait:

> And God will wipe away every tear from their eyes; there shall be no more death, nor sorrow, nor crying. There shall be no more pain, for the former things have passed away. … He who overcomes shall inherit all things, and I will be his God and he shall be My son. (Revelation 21:4, 7)

No matter what we endure in this life, if we choose to serve God, the blissful fellowship that will result will make it worthwhile.

So why did God not create a world in which all men are forced to serve Him? Alvin Plantinga answered the question:

> God can create free creatures, but He can't *cause* or *determine* them to do only what is right. For if He does so, they aren't significantly free after all; they do not do what is right *freely*. To create creatures capable of *moral good,* therefore, He must create creatures capable of moral evil; and He can't give these creatures the freedom to perform evil and at the same time prevent them from doing so. [13]

While this might settle the issue, I would contend the question is misguided. The point is not that God lacked the ability to create a world in which freedom of choice does not exist – a world that would be radically different from our own. Rather, the point is that God chose to create *our* world. Therefore, our focus should center on the purpose of creation rather than the details of it. That purpose – which allows man the ability to choose freely to engage in a relationship with God – should thrill our souls. As freewill beings, let us not take this opportunity for granted.

Conclusion

God has not endowed man with the mere appearance of freedom; He has given us the genuine ability to choose to serve Him or to do the opposite. For such freedom to exist, God had to reveal Himself in the perfect way to humanity. He is, thus, near enough that man can know Him if man desires. Nevertheless, God is not so close that man is overwhelmed by His presence. As a result, man is a free moral agent. This characteristic, as much as any other, helps to define humanity. Because we have complete freedom, our actions are not predetermined. Yet our decisions do have consequences. Sin is the obvious result of man's free will, and "the wages of sin is death" (Romans 6:23). Thankfully, our capacity for freedom also allows us to turn to God for help. When we do, our Savior willingly redeems us with His blood (Ephesians 1:7).

Questions for Consideration

1. How does Scripture imply that man has free will?

2. What are some passages that explicitly assert that man is a free moral agent?

3. What is meant by "compatibilism"? How would you respond to this approach to freedom?

4. What is meant by "incompatibilism"?

5. How can God have foreknowledge of man's actions but still allow him to retain his freedom?

6. Why is the concept of "epistemic distance" important?

7. What are some results of freedom?

10

An Emotional Being

Although we do not know the exact events that precipitated the writing of Psalm 42, clearly the author of that text was struggling emotionally. His questions – "Why are you cast down, O my soul? And why are you disquieted within me?" (v. 5) – reveal the presence of inner turmoil in his life. Essentially, the psalmist examined his own life, recognized his soul was downcast, and had the presence of mind to question his psychological status. From this we can conclude that he possessed the ability to both think and feel.

In a broad sense, what can be said about the psalmist also can be said about mankind in general. Like the psalmist, man has the capacity to think and feel. And like the psalmist, man's emotions play a vital role in his well-being. Emotions can cause man's soul to be cast down or to rejoice. Regardless, any adequate description of man must at least acknowledge that he is an emotional being.

In this chapter, we will consider man as an emotional being from several different angles. First, we will define emotions and examine the role they play in man's life. Then, we will turn our attention to the question of whether we have the ability to control our emotions. Having answered that important question, we will consider some passages that provide insight into overcoming the emotional struggles we face. All the while we will seek to affirm that man not only experiences the full range of emotions, but also benefits greatly from having them.

Man's Emotions and the Role They Play

It is one thing to say that man is an emotional being, but it is quite another to clarify what is meant by that statement. In part, it means man possesses strong feelings that often affect his judgment. Sometimes these feelings, or emotions, help man in making good decisions. At other times, however, man's emotions stand in the way of his rational thinking. As Kerry Duke has observed, "Emotions are the driving force behind many of our actions, both good and bad. And while it is true that emotions sometimes hinder rational thought, they also have the ability to stimulate the intellect." [1] To illustrate, someone motivated by genuine love will act with the best interests of others in mind because love "does not seek its own" (1 Corinthians 13:5). On the other hand, someone consumed with fear may allow that emotion to keep him from acting in an appropriate manner (see Matthew 25:24-25).

If our emotions do not always help us to make good decisions, then what purpose do they serve? In part, emotions help us develop our personalities. Carol Sigelman and David Shaffer have described this process:

> As you can see, there is change *and* stability, discontinuity *and* continuity, in the development of the self across the life span. Before adulthood, considerable change occurs. Infants who only dimly perceive that they exist as separate beings become adolescents or young adults who have developed elaborate theories about the workings of personality and who have forged unique, complex identities. [2]

Individual growth and development certainly are aided by positive emotions. And if one conquers negative emotions like worry or pride, those victories also aid in the development of the individual's character.

This leads to the second function of the emotions: They are an integral part of the environment that helps man grow and develop spiritually. To understand this point, one need only imagine what man's decisions would look like if he were totally void of emotions. Regardless of whether the emotions help man to make good decisions, it is at least true that man's choices are more complex because of them. And while we may tend to view this in a negative light, we also could conclude that our emotions provide the type of resistance that often helps us grow stronger. Making this same point, Duke wrote:

> If we always acted rationally upon our knowledge of good and evil, perhaps we would never sin. A substantial drawing power is needed to give man the potential to act irrationally. This pull away from rational behavior is made possible by physical drives and psychological capacities as they interact with one's environment. The emotions constitute an intense force which, when uncontrolled, distort the rational processes of the mind. Had God created us emotionless, purely intellectual beings, we would not experience the necessary level of tension in our choice between good and evil. Without emotions, little if any will power would be needed to avoid sin. The virtue of doing good and the testing aspect of earth life would be lost. [3]

In granting the value of emotions in helping man to develop spiritually, we would do well to take another look at Psalm 42. As was noted previously, the psalmist not only realized his soul was restless, but also wondered why. His evident conclusion, gathered from an examination of the text, was that he lacked confidence in God. Eddie Cloer has explained the connection between overcoming emotional distress and having faith in God in this way: "Sometimes the difficulties that plague us rush forcefully into our minds, producing fears and doubts, taking us into a downward spin. When they fill our minds, we have to chase them away with the assurance that God has not forsaken us." [4] This seems to imply that a connection exists between our relationship with God and the emotions we experience.

That is not to say that all of man's emotional difficulties are linked to his spiritual status, but certainly some, if not many, of our emotional struggles are. As Wayne Jackson has written,

Many of our strictly emotional difficulties are self-induced; they are, in fact, spiritual problems that have gone unresolved in sensitive people; they have escalated to a state where the conscience is tormented egregiously and the subjects simply cannot enjoy a happy, fulfilled life. [5]

But is this the way it must be? Must we allow our lives to be driven by our emotions? Or is it possible to control them?

Can Man Control His Emotions?

Because man experiences the *full* range of emotions, it is paramount that he exercises self-control. This would not necessarily be true if man experienced only positive emotions such as love or joy. But man also must deal with negative emotions such as guilt, worry, fear and anger.

Establishing that man has the capability to control his emotions is as easy as looking at two passages designed to combat uncontrolled anger. (1) Ephesians 4:26 states, "Be angry, and do not sin: do not let the sun go down on your wrath." (2) James 1:19-20 states: "So then, my beloved brethren, let every man be swift to hear, slow to speak, slow to wrath; for the wrath of man does not produce the righteousness of God." In both instances, the text implies that man has the ability to hold his anger in check. In other words, man is to control his emotions; his emotions are not to control him.

Significantly, the Bible not only contains prescriptions for anger, but also provides an example of One who did not allow anger to turn to wrath. According to Mark 3:5, Jesus, realizing the religious leaders of His day were seeking to catch Him in some violation of the Sabbath day law, "looked around at them with anger." But this strong emotion did not distract our Lord from the task at hand. Rather than allowing His anger to become wrath, He simply turned from them and healed a man's withered hand. This account, like the aforementioned passages concerning anger, demonstrates that man can control his emotions. An angry person may well experience that emotion and still remain in control. "It is not the anger, therefore, that is sinful, but the incorrect, unchristian expression of it." [6]

This principle actually can be applied to many of the emotional struggles common to man. In addition to anger, for example, man has the ability to conquer anxiety and worry. Jesus said, "Therefore I say to you, do not worry about your life" (Matthew 6:25), and the apostle Paul wrote that Christians are to "be anxious for nothing, but in every-thing by prayer and supplication, with thanksgiving, let your requests be made known to God" (Philippians 4:6). The battle with worry that so many people fight each day is one that can be won. Instead of fret-ting because of past mistakes or fainting at the prospects of the future, men and women have the ability to focus on and handle the present situation. And this, according to our Lord, is sufficient (Matthew 6:34).

The Bible also describes how man can overcome guilt (2 Corinthians 7:10-11; 1 John 1:9) and fear (4:18). As with anger and worry, one key to handling guilt and fear is to revise the thinking process. With guilt, one must genuinely repent of and confess the sinful action. With fear, one must replace the negative emotion with a positive one. In both cases, the individual must examine his life and refocus his mind. The example of how Paul and Silas dealt with their unjust imprisonment in Philippi illustrates this process. Rather than dwelling on their wrongful treatment and allowing negative emotions to consume their thoughts, Paul and Silas passed the time "praying and singing hymns to God" (Acts 16:25). It is little wonder that the apostle Paul later wrote to the Philippians, "I have learned in whatever state I am, to be content" (Philippians 4:11).

So is it possible for man to control his emotions? The Bible clearly affirms that it is not only possible, but necessary. But in order to do so, man must realize he possesses the ability to experience emotions without allowing those strong feelings to rule his life. Without this understand-ing, emotionally misguided behavior will almost certainly result. That is when man must realize the importance of changing his thought process. As Paul L. Cates has observed, "The root causes of emotions like anger, guilt, anxiety, worry, fear, resentment, and sadness should be identified and the person be helped to understand how to change thoughts and behaviors to help eliminate or control the negative emotions." [7]

Passages That Help Overcome Emotional Difficulties

Because Scripture is capable of equipping man "for every good work" (2 Timothy 3:17), it is not surprising to find certain passages designed to help man face and overcome the emotional difficulties of life. One of the most well-known of these passages is Psalm 23. Within that familiar text, we are reassured of God's presence, provisions and protection, and we are told about the peace that God's followers may enjoy. Describing how this beautiful psalm has affected man, Henry Ward Beecher wrote:

> It has charmed more griefs to rest than all the philosophy of the world. It has remanded to their dungeon more felon thoughts, more black doubts, more thieving sorrows, than the sands on the sea-shore. It has comforted the noble host of the poor. It has sung courage to the army of the disappointed. It has poured balm and consolation into the heart of the sick, of captives in dungeons, of widows in their pinching griefs, of orphans in their loneliness. Dying soldiers have died easier as it was read to them; ghastly hospitals have been illuminated; it has visited the prisoner, and broken his chains, and like Peter's angel, led him forth in imagination, and sung him back to his home again. [8]

According to Psalm 23, we can face the most difficult of situations – "the valley of the shadow of death" – because our God will not forsake us. And when we believe God is doing what He can to ease our burdens, our struggle – although still very real – is much less difficult. This psalm is able to help us overcome emotional difficulties, wrote Charles L. Allen, "because it tells that above all the strife and fears, the hungers and weaknesses of mankind, there is a Shepherd." And it reminds us that our Shepherd is one "who knows his sheep one by one, who is abundantly able to provide, who guides and protects and at the close of the day opens the door to the sheepfold – the house not made with hands." [9]

Another passage to which individuals may turn for comfort is Matthew 5:3-12. Collectively known as the Beatitudes, these verses address the various states of man required for genuine happiness. Those struggling with negative emotions would do well to consider our Lord's blueprint for building a joyful life. As Hugo McCord has written, "Truly happy people have learned that the principles underlying the eight beatitudes of Jesus are basic, eternal, and sure. When these standards are carefully laid in men's hearts and woven into their lives, happiness is 'sure-fire.' There are no misses." [10]

Conclusion

Man is a being fraught with emotion. Some of these emotions are positive and desirable, while others are potentially dangerous. But all of them are valuable. If nothing more, man benefits by facing the emotional challenges of life. Although our emotions are sometimes difficult to bear, we must never forget that God is willing and able to help us through the difficulties of life. As Charles Brewer noted, "If God can supply our physical needs, we believe that He can also meet the needs of the spirit." [11] For this we – as emotional beings – should be thankful. Perhaps we do not always rely upon God to help us handle our emotions properly, but we should remember that the God who created us in His own image understands our emotional struggles and has made us so that we can overcome them. When we do so, we grow closer to God.

Questions for Consideration

1. How can Psalm 42:5 be used to prove that man is an emotional being?

2. How do emotions affect man's ability to make decisions?

3. What part do man's emotions play in helping him to develop spiritually?

4. In what way are some emotional difficulties linked to man's spiritual status?

5. What two passages imply that man has the ability to control his anger?

6. What role, if any, does self-examination play in overcoming emotional difficulties?

7. How could Psalm 23 be used to help someone overcome emotional difficulties?

8. How could Matthew 5:3-12 be used to help someone overcome emotional difficulties?

11

A Religious
Being

I t is not possible to examine the societies of the world without noticing the religious tendencies of men and women. Regardless of culture, time frame or location, individuals throughout history have consistently engaged in religious behavior. That does not mean their observable religious expressions have been uniform or even similar, for they have not; the great differences in religious beliefs and practices of Hindus and Christians, for example, are easy to recognize. Nevertheless, the idea that man is subservient to a higher power seems to prevail. Consider the following from the book *Religions of the World:*

> *Wherever people are found, there too is religion.* Occasionally, religion is hard to find or pin down, but from the great metropolitan capitals to the least developed areas of the world, there are temples, pyramids, megaliths, and other monuments societies have raised at tremendous expense as expressions of their religions. Even when we explore the backwaters of time in prehistoric civilizations, we find alters, cave paintings, and special burials that point to our religious

nature. Indeed, no other phenomenon is so pervasive, so
consistent from society to society, as is the search for gods. [1]

Given this fact, it would not be a mistake to say man is a religious being.
But what exactly do we mean when we say man is a religious being? Do we mean he is religious in the same way that he is a physical
specimen? Are we saying his religious beliefs are inseparable from his
nature? Or are we saying his religious beliefs are the product of his
environment? If religious beliefs are inseparable from man's nature,
then we must be able to explain why so many different religions are
practiced in our world today. We also must be able to explain why some
people do not seem to be religious at all. But if those beliefs are the
product of man's environment, then we must account for the origin of
particular religious practices and explain the universality of religion.

Rather than affirming that man owes his religious nature either to
his birth or his society, we will learn how man's religious nature stems
from both. In the sense that man is a being within whom God has placed
a spirit and an idea of eternity (Ecclesiastes 3:11), it is correct to say
that man is innately religious. In the sense that man is a being to whom
God gave the ability to reason, it is correct to say that man's evaluation
and reaction to his environment lead to his religious behavior. The fact
that God does not force man to believe or act in a particular way can
be deduced from the divergent religious practices in our world; the
fact that He endows man with religious desire can be gathered from
the universal existence of religion.

This chapter will consider man as a religious being by seeking answers
to the following questions: What does it mean to be religious? Why
should man seek to be religious? Are all attempts at religious behavior
the same? And what are some hindrances to man's attempt to live as
a religious being? Having considered answers to these questions, we
will conclude by asserting that an adequate description of man's nature
is impossible without including the idea that he is a religious being.

What Does It Mean to Be Religious?
The term "religion" is used quite frequently in our conversations. Nev-
ertheless, it is a difficult term to define. As authors George Abernathy and
Thomas Langford put it, "Religion is a pervasive and almost universal

phenomenon in human societies. Yet one of the striking facts about the word *religion* is that, although we use it without hesitation, we have great difficulty in telling others what we mean by it." [2] Perhaps this is because of "the wide variety of religious beliefs and practices found in the world." [3] Nevertheless, numerous definitions for religion have been offered. These definitions span from Paul Tillich's idea that religion is that which is of "ultimate concern" to William James' suggestion that religion "consists of the belief that there is an unseen order, and that our supreme good lies in harmoniously adjusting ourselves thereto." [4] Tillich is correct in claiming that religion is to be of "ultimate concern." Jesus certainly taught us to put the kingdom above all else (Matthew 6:33; Luke 14:26-27). But for the purpose of a definition, this description is lacking because it does not specify what should be most important and why it should be so. Likewise, James' assertion that religion involves the recognition of an order higher than man and an effort to conform man's life to that order is also accurate – but it stops short of affirming the exclusive nature of that order. Both attempts fail to make mention of either God or His plan. This is a fatal mistake.

So what is religion? Religion is the term used to describe man's attempt to live in a manner that is pleasing in God's sight. Religion is based on two foundational assertions: (1) Man must recognize his deep need for God, and (2) God has made provisions for man by revealing His exclusive will to him. To say that man is a religious being is to say he is seeking to order his life according to God's plan. If he falls short of the revealed plan, man's religion is useless (James 1:26). But if he lives acceptably, his religion can properly be described as pure (v. 27).

Why Should Man Seek to Be Religious?

The question of why man should seek to be religious is perhaps the most significant question that could be asked. And generally speaking, the answer is obvious. As a spiritual being, man must make an effort to understand and prepare for that which succeeds his physical existence. The suggestion that God has put eternity in men's hearts (Ecclesiastes 3:11) seems to support this. Thus, James Burton Coffman wrote, "There is in every human heart a longing for eternal life and the instinctive certainty of it." [5]

And while our answer in the previous paragraph to the question might be sufficient, there seems to be several other reasons why men should be religious. For instance, men should be religious in order to help them overcome the problem of physical suffering. The physical difficulties we face are trying, and we must not fail to notice that those sufferings are much easier to bear if we keep them in the proper perspective. Paul was doing this very thing when he wrote, "For I consider that the sufferings of this present time are not worthy to be compared with the glory which shall be revealed in us" (Romans 8:18). Stating similar sentiments to the Corinthians, he added:

> Therefore we do not lose heart. Even though our outward man is perishing, yet the inward man is being renewed day by day. For our light affliction, which is but for a moment, is working for us a far more exceeding and eternal weight of glory, while we do not look at the things which are seen, but at the things which are not seen. For the things which are seen are temporary, but the things which are not seen are eternal. (2 Corinthians 4:16-18)

An additional reason to be religious is the undeniable reality of God's existence. This fact was made plain to the Gentiles of Rome who, according to Romans 1:18, were guilty of suppressing the truth in unrighteousness, for they ignored the clear evidence of God's existence and power. Paul went on:

> For since the creation of the world His invisible attributes are clearly seen, being understood by the things that are made, even His eternal power and Godhead, so that they are without excuse, because, although they knew God, they did not glorify Him as God, nor were thankful, but became futile in their thoughts, and their foolish hearts were darkened. (Romans 1:20-21)

According to the inspired apostle, the very world in which we live stands as a testimony to God's existence and power. Moses E. Lard wrote: "It is easy to understand how the notion of God's power is obtained from the works of creation. These works are an effect, and as such they must have had an adequate cause." [6] Man needs only to examine the world – the effect – to recognize that the wonderful creation arose from a source much greater than he. No wonder the psalmist proclaimed: "The heavens declare the glory of God; And the firmament shows His handiwork" (Psalm 19:1). Incidentally, the universality of religious behavior certainly could be attributed, at least in part, to man's ability to recognize God from nature.

One also could argue that man should seek to be religious in order to express his thanksgiving for all that God has done. As the giver of every good and perfect gift (James 1:17), God is worthy of man's praise. Religion avails man the opportunity to express his thanksgiving. As the beautiful Psalm 100 states, we should "be thankful to Him, and bless His name" (v. 4).

Religion also provides man with the motivation to avoid worldly behavior. The example of Moses, found in Hebrews 11:24-26, illustrates this point:

> By faith Moses, when he became of age, refused to be called the son of Pharaoh's daughter, choosing rather to suffer affliction with the people of God than to enjoy the passing pleasures of sin, esteeming the reproach of Christ greater riches than the treasures in Egypt; for he looked to the reward.

Why did Moses avoid the sinful pleasures available to him? He did so because he judged that avoiding the reproach associated with sin was more important than enjoying momentary pleasure. God wants those who follow Him to "live soberly, righteously, and godly in the present age, looking for the blessed hope and glorious appearing of our great God and Savior Jesus Christ" (Titus 2:12-13).

Are All Attempts at Religious Behavior the Same?

Having provided a working definition for religion and having suggested some of the reasons why man should *seek* to be religious, we now must consider whether all attempts at religious behavior are of the same quality. Consulting the Scriptures, we find a definite no. In a general sense, any attempt to behave religiously that fails to adhere to Jesus' plan falls short. This is true because He is "the way, the truth, and the life. No one comes to the Father except through [Him]" (John 14:6). Or as He said in John 10:9, "I am the door. If anyone enters by Me, he will be saved, and will go in and out and find pasture." The efforts of any religious group that denies Jesus' position as Son of God are therefore ruled out.

In a more specific sense, however, not everyone who claims to follow Jesus is pleasing to Him (Matthew 7:21-23). The Bible speaks of those who worshiped God vainly (15:8-9) and ignorantly (Acts 17:22-23), and it contrasts proper and improper worship (compare Matthew 6:1-4 with Mark 12:41-44). If we learn anything from this, it is that we must structure our efforts to please God around His desires. At the same time, it reminds us that not all attempts to act religiously are equal.

What Hinders Man's Attempts to Live as a Religious Being?

We have established that it is not enough to just be religious. In fact, it is not even enough to claim to be a follower of Christ. We must do more than simply pay lip service to the Savior. We must be obedient to Him (Hebrews 5:9). But in order to do that, we must overcome certain things that hinder us.

Among the many things we must overcome in order to live religious lives is selfishness. Lying at the root of every conceivable sin, selfishness keeps man from doing the will of God. As long as man is content to do as he chooses, God's plan for man's behavior will be of little importance. The remedy for this behavior is to live a selfless life (Philippians 2:3-4) and to overcome the tendency to fall in love with the world rather than with the Savior (1 John 2:15-17). Man certainly must be on guard lest he be cheated "through philosophy and empty deceit, according to the tradition of men, according to the basic principles of the world, and not according to Christ" (Colossians 2:8). We must never forget that "the world through wisdom did not know God" (1 Corinthians 1:21). Consequently, we must not place more stock in man's intellectual suggestions than we do in God's Word.

Conclusion

It is not possible to describe man adequately without discussing him as a religious being. Perhaps this is true because when man acts in accordance with God's plan, he is at his best. Regardless, it cannot be denied that men throughout the world commonly seek to glorify and honor a higher power. By doing so, they show to the world that they are religious beings.

Questions for Consideration

1. What does the prevalence of religious behavior in the world say about man's religious nature?

2. Is man's religious behavior innate, learned or both? Explain.

3. What is meant by the term "religion"?

4. How can religion help with the problem of physical suffering?

5. In what way is God's existence and power obvious?

6. What passage would you use to show that all attempts at religious behavior are not equal?

7. How can trust in the world's wisdom hinder a person religiously?

12

A Mortal/
Immortal Being

The trials faced by the biblical character Job are well-known. As the result of losing his wealth, his children, his servants, his health, and the support of his wife, Job lamented his birth (Job 3:3-11). But it was not until after several exchanges with his friends that Job asked one of the most important questions ever uttered: "If a man dies, shall he live again?" (14:14). Job had no reason to question the reality of death. He had, of course, just endured the deaths of his children and his servants. Recognizing the mortality of man, Job was not looking for a confirmation of death, but for a reason to hope in the face of it. He realized man is a mortal being – but he clung to the idea that man is immortal.

There is little dispute in our world about the mortality of man, perhaps because our experiences confirm "it is appointed for men to die once" (Hebrews 9:27). As physical beings, humans possess material bodies that perish. Given this truth, it would seem the subject of death would be one we all understand completely. However, "we know so little of death, that it is at once the most obvious and the least well-known fact of human experience." [1] Whether that statement is entirely true is certainly debatable. But what is not up for debate is the fact that man's

knowledge about death apart from God's Word does not come close
to matching what he can know about it by studying the Scriptures.

Similarly, man's knowledge about what lies beyond the veil of death
is often hindered by his unwillingness to examine the subject in the
light of God's Word. When we avail ourselves to Scripture, we will,
like Job, seriously consider whether death is the end. And having done
so, we will conclude with Paul: "If in this life only we have hope in
Christ, we are of all men the most pitiable" (1 Corinthians 15:19).

The intention of this chapter is to affirm that man is both a mortal and
an immortal being. Man is mortal in the sense that his physical body
is subject to death; man is immortal in the sense that his soul lives on
after his material body has perished. In order to deal with this topic
justly, we must take a closer look at death. We will make an effort to
better understand not only why death affects man, but also what man
can do to better cope with death. That effort will necessarily involve a
consideration of what the Bible says about man's eternal nature. We will
then affirm the conclusion drawn by Paul when he considered man's
physical demise. He wrote with both simplicity and power:

> For we know that if our earthly house, this tent, is de-
> stroyed, we have a building from God, a house not made
> with hands, eternal in the heavens. For in this we groan,
> earnestly desiring to be clothed with our habitation which
> is from heaven. (2 Corinthians 5:1-2)

Man Is a Mortal Being

We generally make an effort to avoid certain subjects, particularly
those we find unpleasant. The subject of death often falls squarely into
this category. Perhaps it is because of the emotions commonly associated with death. For all practical purposes, it is nearly impossible to
think about death without thinking either about loved ones who have
died or about our own eventual demise. William J. Abraham recognized
this and wrote:

> Death is not a pleasant topic; for most people it is very
> naturally a forbidding and emotional matter. After all,
> death can have a devastating effect upon us, as happens

when someone very close to us dies. Moreover, when
we stop to think about our own death, there is often a
sense of fear and mystery which can leave us confused
and uncertain. [2]

But a comprehensive discussion about man's nature would be impossible without mentioning the subject of death.
What is death? Like so many other terms discussed in previous chapters, it may be easier to point to an example of death than to define the term. But the difficulties associated with providing an acceptable definition for the term "death" do not negate the possibility of doing so – an important consideration particularly when we realize that the definition one gives to death also affects one's definition of life. For example, Robert Veatch has defined death as "a complete change in the status of a living entity characterized by the irreversible loss of those characteristics that are essentially significant to it." [3] Although not stated in this vague definition, the door is obviously left open to argue that one is dead when he or she loses certain characteristics generally associated with functioning humans. A chief characteristic around which the discussion often revolves is consciousness. Consequently, if one accepts the above definition, it would be difficult to argue against those who claim that when a being lacks the ability to maintain consciousness, he or she is actually dead.

While it might be tempting to equate death with the irreversible loss of necessary bodily functions, we must proceed very carefully for two important reasons. (1) We have no reason to think that the loss of a physical characteristic that provides value to human life is the same as the loss of life itself. This point has been made forcefully by David J. Mayo and Daniel Winkler in their essay "Euthanasia and the Transition From Life to Death":

> It is enormously plausible to suggest that one of the conditions for a human life *having value* is the possibility of consciousness. But, while the possibility of consciousness seems quite clearly to be a condition of human life *having value,* that is not to say that it is a condition of a human being *having life.* [4]

(2) We have no right to change the definition of death provided to us in Scripture: "For as the body without the spirit is dead, so faith without works is dead also" (James 2:26).

Admittedly, this definition does not solve the debate, because it does not specify when the spirit departs from the body. But it does provide a foundational principle (i.e., a person is not dead until his spirit departs from his body). But when, specifically, does this take place? The Bible does not explicitly state the exact moment, but it does provide us with information that is quite helpful. Namely, it tells us when life begins. This is significant because of the relationship that exists between the terms "life" and "death." The Bible asserts death occurs at the moment the spirit departs from the body; it seems to follow, then, that because a being that is not dead must be alive, life begins at the moment the physical is joined to the spiritual. According to Job 3:3, that moment is at conception. Considering this, it seems reasonable to say that death – the moment in which the spirit departs from the body – occurs when the body ceases to function in totality. Regardless, we must be careful to avoid putting ourselves in the place of God (see Genesis 50:19; Job 1:21).

How should we view death? Having set forth God's definition of death, we would do well to consider how death is to be understood. D.A. Carson's comments illustrate why the question is so important. He wrote:

> We know that we are not immune, but there is a suppressed hope that pretends we are. And when our child dies, or our spouse; when we see a loved one wasting away from a painful disease, or observe a brilliant mind disintegrating before our eyes; when we ourselves suddenly face the most appalling pain or incapacity, with no prospect of relief, then our pretentions rush forward in another form: Why is God doing this? Though it is blasphemous to think it, our whole being cries out that this is unfair of him, that our grief and pain are disproportionate to our sin, and that we have been abandoned. [5]

So how are we to view death? We must view death at least three ways. (1) We must view death as punishment for the sin of man. Paul wrote to the Romans, "For the wages of sin is death, but the gift of God is eternal life in Christ Jesus our Lord" (Romans 6:23). Earlier in that same book, Paul pointed out that "through one man sin entered the world, and death through sin, and thus death spread to all men, because all sinned" (5:12). We cannot understand death without developing some understanding of how the righteous God views sin.

(2) We must view death as inescapable. According to Ecclesiastes 3:2, there is "a time to be born, And a time to die." Death is, as the writer of Hebrews asserts, an appointment that all men will keep (9:27). And the psalmist may have put it best when he asked: "What man can live and not see death? Can he deliver his life from the power of the grave?" (Psalm 89:48). No matter what man might want, and despite his best efforts to avoid it, death still occurs. Emily Dickinson verbalized this at the beginning of her poem "The Chariot": "Because I could not stop for Death, He kindly stopped for me." [6]

(3) We must view death as the passage to eternity. Rather than looking at death with fear, the Christian can face death confidently in the same way Paul did. As he neared the end of his life, Paul wrote to Timothy: "I have fought the good fight, I have finished the race, I have kept the faith. Finally, there is laid up for me the crown of righteousness, which the Lord, the righteous Judge, will give to me on that Day, and not to me only but also to all who have loved His appearing" (2 Timothy 4:7-8). Paul was able to face death confidently because of the redemptive work of Jesus. According to Hebrews 2:14, Jesus came to the earth as a man so "that through death He might destroy him who had the power of death, that is, the devil." And just like Paul, we, because of the death of Christ, can ask: "O Death, where is your sting? O Hades, where is your victory?" (1 Corinthians 15:55).

If any questions existed as to whether man is a mortal being, one would need look no further than to the all-too-present reality of death to assuage those doubts. It is important to recognize that individuals throughout recorded history have readily noticed and accepted death. Man's physical body has a beginning on earth, and it will also have an end. Thus, man is undeniably mortal.

Man Is an Immortal Being

The claim that man is immortal certainly is more controversial than the claim that he is mortal. The terms "mortal" and "immortal" should not be considered contradictory, as they have different points of reference. Man is mortal in the sense that his physical body will not last. Man is immortal in the sense that his soul will live eternally.

The idea that man's soul will exist long after his body ceases to live is upheld throughout the biblical text. Whether we point to Job's consideration of the fact (Job 14:14), David's assertion that he would go to be with his child who died (2 Samuel 12:23), or Jesus' promise to prepare a heavenly place for the faithful (John 14:1-3), numerous passages support the idea that man's soul lives on after his death. Peter put it plainly when he wrote:

> Blessed be the God and Father of our Lord Jesus Christ, who according to His abundant mercy has begotten us again to a living hope through the resurrection of Jesus Christ from the dead, to an inheritance incorruptible and undefiled and that does not fade away, reserved in heaven for you. (1 Peter 1:3-4)

It is worth noting that the concept of individual immortality is not just limited to those who believe the Bible. Just as individuals throughout history and across cultures have exhibited religious tendencies, many of those same individuals have left behind evidence indicating their belief in some form of life after death. And while the widespread belief of a thing does not necessitate its validity, it does beg for an explanation.

Explanations notwithstanding, the concept of man's immortality is inseparably linked to Jesus' resurrection from the dead. Wilbur M. Smith made this point in the following helpful passage:

> Not only was the resurrection of Christ one of the two great foundational stones of the gospel, but on the fact of Christ's resurrection almost every great Christian theme seems to rest. Paul says that it was by His resurrection that Christ was declared to be the Son of God; it was for our justification that He was raised. We are assured of a judgment to come by the fact that God raised Christ from the dead. Our one great assurance of being raised ourselves from the dead is

in the conviction that Christ is the first fruits of them who sleep, and that if God raised Him, He will also raise us from the dead. If Christ has not been raised from the dead, our preaching is vain, our faith is vain, we are yet in our sins, and those that have fallen asleep have perished. [7]

This does not mean everyone will accept that man is an immortal being, for they will not. Some have actually tried to argue that the concept of immortality fails to make sense. William J. Abraham wrote that he found it "impossible to preserve the thread of personal identity through the drastic changes necessary to take one through an intermediate state to ultimate resurrection." [8] What this objection fails to consider is that man's real identity is not linked to his outward appearance (1 Samuel 16:7). Although man's body may perish, his identity – his soul – continues to exist. Thus, we may correctly describe man as an immortal being.

Conclusion

Although it may sound contradictory to describe man as both mortal and immortal, both terms are necessary to adequately describe the nature of man. Because our physical bodies are perishing, we must make every effort to use the limited time we have on earth to prepare for the eternity to come.

Questions for Consideration

1. What is the significance of the question raised in Job 14:14?

2. What could hinder one from knowing about man's immortal nature?

3. Why do we often avoid talking about death?

4. How would you define the term "death"?

5. Why is it dangerous to define death in terms of the possession of essential characteristics?

6. How are the meanings of the terms "life" and "death" linked?

7. How should the Christian view death?

8. What are some passages that assert man's immortal nature?

9. How is the resurrection of Christ linked to man's immortal nature?

13

❧

A Hopeful Being

A fter witnessing the terrible events that transpired during the fall of Jerusalem to the Babylonians, the prophet Jeremiah wrote:

> My eyes fail with tears, My heart is troubled; My bile is poured on the ground Because of the destruction of the daughter of my people, Because the children and the infants Faint in the streets of the city. They say to their mothers, "Where is grain and wine?" As they swoon like the wounded In the streets of the city, As their life is poured out In their mothers' bosom. (Lamentations 2:11-12)

Although Jeremiah's words seem to indicate he had lost all hope, that was not the case. He went on to write: "Through the LORD's mercies we are not consumed, Because His compassions fail not. They are new every morning; Great is Your faithfulness. 'The LORD is my portion,' says my soul, 'Therefore I hope in Him!' " (3:22-24). Rather than giving up, Jeremiah continued to place his trust in God despite being faced with great difficulty. His hope in God seems to have enabled him to go on.

Like Jeremiah, individuals today need something to keep them going in the face of adversity; and like Jeremiah, that something is hope. In this chapter, we will consider man as a hopeful being. In so doing, we will seek to establish a working definition of hope, attempt to depict what man's life might look like without hope, and set forth a biblical basis for the concept of hope. All the while, we will affirm that hope plays a definitive role in making man what he is: a being made in God's image who is seeking to prepare for the coming eternity.

What Is Hope?

As the term is commonly used, the word "hope" refers to the sincere expectation of a particular thing or event. Frequently, the term is used to describe what individuals *want*. Scripture, however, regularly links man's hope to God and the redemptive work of Jesus Christ. When used in this manner, hope transforms something that is far from sure into something in which man can have confidence. Consequently, hope can strengthen man by enabling him to see beyond the moment.

The hope of the Christian cannot be separated from the resurrection of Jesus. In fact, it is the resurrection that provides us with the hope that man's existence is more than just the physical. Because Jesus is living, our hope is living – which is why Paul wrote to those who denied the resurrection: "If in this life only we have hope in Christ, we are of all men the most pitiable" (1 Corinthians 15:19). And that is why Peter affirmed that God "has begotten us again to a living hope through the resurrection of Jesus Christ from the dead" (1 Peter 1:3).

Hope, then, is the confident expectation of divine deliverance from the difficulties associated with living in a world filled with sin and sorrow. That does not mean the Christian fails to hope for God's mercy in this life, for he certainly does. As Rudolf Bultmann put it,

> The life of the righteous is grounded in hope. To have hope, to have a future, is a sign that all things are well with us. This hope is naturally directed to God. It is naturally referred to most frequently when man is in trouble and hopes that God will deliver him and help him. [1]

But deliverance from physical adversity is not the chief end of the Christian's hope. Instead, that hope is only realized in heaven (Colossians 1:5).

Defining hope and demonstrating its proper inclusion as a characteristic of humanity are two different things. When we compare hope to some of the other qualities assigned to man in this book, such as man's physical nature, it seems that hope must be classified differently. After all, man certainly cannot help but possess a physical body, but he can choose to refrain from being hopeful. Hope, then, does not appear to be inherently attached to man at birth. Nevertheless, the concept of hope is intrinsic to Christianity. As the writer of Hebrews put it, hope serves as "an anchor of the soul, both sure and steadfast" (6:19). This leads us to conclude that while hope may not be a primary quality of man, it is certainly of primary importance to his spirituality. Thus, regardless of whether man actually is a hopeful being, he *should be.*

Life Without Hope

Although it certainly does not have to be the case, many individuals live what might properly be described as hopeless lives. Generally speaking, a spirit of resignation dominates a life without hope. Those who fall into this class, regardless of whether they realize it, might properly be described as existentialists. These individuals fail to find objective meaning in life. Instead, they believe the meaning of life is subjectively tied to the freedom of each individual. The philosophy of *existentialism* is not limited to those who deny God's existence. In fact, one of existentialism's most notable proponents was Søren Kierkegaard (1813–1855). Advocating his position, Kierkegaard wrote:

> It is impossible to live artistically before one has made up one's mind to abandon hope; for hope precludes self-limitation. It is a very beautiful sight to see a man put out to sea with the fair wind of hope, and one may even use the opportunity to be taken in tow; but one should never permit hope to be taken aboard one's own ship, least of all as a pilot; for hope is a faithless shipmaster. [2]

Kierkegaard's position is typical of those who reject the idea that anything outside of man's own individual actions provides meaning to life. Perhaps more revealing, however, is the description of existentialism provided by the atheist Jean-Paul Sartre (1905–1980):

If existence really does precede essence, then there is no explaining things away by reference to a fixed and given human nature. In other words, there is no determinism, man is free, man is freedom. On the other hand, if God does not exist, we find no values or commands to turn to which legitimize our conduct. So, in the bright realm of values, we have no excuse behind us, nor justification before us. We are alone, with no excuses. [3]

In Sartre's position, value only exists because man exists; good is what man determines it to be. And without God in the picture, not only is man free to determine his own course, but he is doomed to do so. As a result, placing hope in anything beyond man's own ability becomes impossible. Man is therefore left to face the difficulties of life without any hope of reprieve. It could be said that man exists, but that is about all. No wonder Paul tried to prevent the Thessalonians from having "sorrow as others who have no hope" (1 Thessalonians 4:13).

The Basis of Hope

Thankfully, those who follow Jesus Christ need not place their hope only in their own abilities. Christians not only have reasons to believe in God, Jesus, and the truthfulness of Scripture, but they also possess a basis, provided by those reasons, for the sincere and confident expectation of relief and deliverance from the struggles associated with this life. In fact, Scripture consistently emphasizes areas in which man should hope and provides numerous reasons *why* man should hope. When man places his hope in the places designated in Scripture, he benefits greatly from the possession of that hope. Man's hope helps to free him from the dread of difficulty. Paul made this point when he outlined how man should be "eagerly waiting for the adoption, the redemption of our body" (Romans 8:23) and wrote, "For we were saved in this hope" (v. 24). This explains why he was later able to write, "For to me, to live is Christ, and to die is gain" (Philippians 1:21). When one has the hope associated with Christianity, death is nothing more than the entrance to eternal reward.

So where should man place his hope? This chart identifies several notable areas:

Man Should Hope In ...

- God .... Psalm 42:5
- God's Word .... Psalm 119:81
- God's promises .... Psalm 119:166-168
- God's glory .... Romans 5:1-5
- God's truthfulness .... Titus 1:2
- God's power .... 1 Peter 1:3-5

The result of hope properly placed is, as the wise man wrote, gladness (Proverbs 10:28). This means that a man who is hopeful not only has the ability to look forward to that which follows his physical life, but that he is also well-equipped to face the difficulties of his life. If we had no other reason, this one would be enough to include hope in the list of qualities essential to man. Man needs hope, and God has provided it.

The Result of Hope

When man possesses the kind of hope described in Scripture, at least three conditions result. (1) He realizes that there is more to his existence than the physical. Rather than being the product of mindless evolution, man views himself as a being with a destiny greater than physical death or destruction. His purpose is to seek the Lord (Acts 17:27), and his desire is to become a child of God so that he might be brought by the Savior to glory (Hebrews 2:10). Hope, thus, enables man to place the trials and difficulties of this physical life in the proper perspective. As difficult as things may be, those who hope for an eternal home in heaven consider the trials of this life to be temporary (2 Corinthians 4:16-18).

(2) He recognizes what is truly valuable. Although we often prize our physical possessions, we are not able to take them with us when we depart from this world (1 Timothy 6:7). Consequently, if one lacks the hope of anything beyond the physical, he or she might slip into despair when considering this fact. King Solomon certainly understood the vanity of such a view when he wrote the following: "Then I hated all my labor in which I had toiled under the sun, because I must leave it to the man who will come after me. And who knows whether he will be wise or a fool?" (Ecclesiastes 2:18-19). The hopeful understand that physical possessions

are subject to decay and theft. Thus, they seek to store "treasures in heaven, where neither moth nor rust destroys and where thieves do not break in and steal" (Matthew 6:20). Man's soul, for those who have hope, is treasured above all the riches this world has to offer (Matthew 16:26).

(3) He relies upon the Savior. Those who have hope trust that Jesus will do as He promised His apostles and return to claim the faithful (John 14:1-4). Consequently, the hopeful seek to live in a manner that anticipates the Lord's coming. Rather than dreading that day, men with hope are able to say, as John said, "Even so, come, Lord Jesus!" (Revelation 22:20).

Conclusion

The person who lives in hope is better suited to overcome trials and difficulties than the individual who is hopeless. This is true because hope provides man with resolve. We would do well to realize the important role hope plays in man's life, and we would benefit greatly by making an extra effort to fulfill the prayer in which the apostle Paul prayed:

> … that you may know what is the hope of His calling, what are the riches of the glory of His inheritance in the saints, and what is the exceeding greatness of His power toward us who believe, according to the working of His mighty power which He worked in Christ when He raised Him from the dead and seated Him at His right hand in the heavenly places, far above all principality and power and might and dominion, and every name that is named, not only in this age but also in that which is to come. (Ephesians 1:18-21)

Only when we realize hope is available to man because of the life, death and resurrection of Jesus will we fully appreciate what God has done for humanity. Not only did God send His Son to the earth because of His great love (John 3:16), but He allowed His Son to "taste death for everyone" (Hebrews 2:9). The redemption man so desperately needs is found in Christ Jesus (Ephesians 1:7), and man has the wonderful opportunity to obey Him (Hebrews 5:9). When we do so, we are washed from our sins by His blood (Revelation 1:5; Acts 22:16), we become new creations (2 Corinthians 5:17), and we are able to live in hope rather than in dread. Let us be thankful that man is a hopeful being!

Questions for Consideration

1. What does Lamentations 3:22-24 tell us about Jeremiah's frame of mind?

2. What does the word "hope" mean?

3. What is the difference between the way hope is used in the Bible and the way the term is used otherwise?

4. In what way is man's hope linked to the resurrection of Jesus?

5. How does Colossians 1:5 help us understand the Christian's hope?

6. What does the term "existentialism" mean?

7. Why is existentialism a hopeless philosophy?

8. What are some areas in which man should hope?

9. How does understanding the connection between God's scheme of redemption and hope help man to appreciate all that God has done?

10. What can you do because of hope?

Afterword

W e began this study by asking the following question: What is man? In hopes of arriving at a definitive answer, we have considered various characteristics that humanity seems to possess. These qualities certainly include the four areas mentioned in Luke's descriptive statement regarding Jesus' growth and development (Luke 2:52). Therefore, like Jesus, man is an intellectual being, a physical being, a spiritual being, and a social being. Although these four areas seem comprehensive, they do not exhaust everything that man is. As our study has shown, man is even more.

Some traits can be associated with humanity in general. Man, for example, possesses the capacity to freely choose his actions. He has the ability to obey God, and he has the ability to disobey. His decisions are not forced upon him. But with this freedom also comes responsibility. Consequently, man is held accountable for what he does. Because of this, men and women are properly subject to criticism on the basis of their actions. As Paul reminded the Galatians, "Do not be deceived, God is not mocked; for whatever a man sows, that he will also reap" (Galatians 6:7).

As accountable beings, men and women must guard against selfish behavior. Particular care must be given to avoiding the temptation to gratify the flesh (1 Corinthians 6:18-20). Man must make an effort to seek what is best for both himself and others (1 Thessalonians 5:15). His emotional composition must likewise be recognized. He must come to understand that true happiness, as this study has shown, is not derived from the pursuits of this world. Rather, man is only fulfilled when he embraces the purpose for which he was created (cf. Ecclesiastes 12:13; Acts 17:27; Ephesians 2:10).

It should also be noted that other qualities are possible for humanity to possess, although they are not always present. For example, all men have the ability to hope. Nevertheless, hope is not present in all men. Many individuals are unprepared for eternity. Some exist in this state by their own choice; others lack hope because they have never been told about the Savior. When faced with great tragedy, these individuals have no foundation upon which to stand. Those who recognize that this world is temporary, however, are better prepared to endure the storms of life. Man can and certainly should be a hopeful being, for biblical hope is sustaining.

If this study has taught us anything, it has taught us that man's nature is extremely complex. We cannot easily describe man as being simply *this* or *that*. Rather, man is the result of all of the qualities that have been discussed in this book and more. Because this is true, we must guard against isolating particular aspects of man and exalting them over others. Man is who he is because of his total composition. Is he physical? Yes. Is he spiritual? Certainly. But again, he is more. Above all, man is a being made in God's image (Genesis 1:27). Perhaps this fact, as much as anything else, should serve to motivate us as we give serious consideration to the nature of man.

Glossary

Compatibilism: the approach to free will that asserts man is free if he has the ability to choose one viable course of action (so long as he is not forced to do so).

Comprehensive: complete; used with reference to an ethical approach that seeks to concern itself with both the end of one's actions as well as the means.

Deontological: the approach to ethics that is based upon one's duty; it is concerned primarily with what motivates one to act.

Egoism: an ethical approach that is based upon the feelings of an individual.

Epistemic Distance: the knowledge gap that exists between God and humanity; God's separation from man is far enough so as to allow humans to possess free will but near enough so as to elicit devotion.

Euthyphro Dilemma: the supposed dilemma, recorded by Plato, wherein one is forced to choose whether goodness precedes deity or results from the divine decree.

Existentialism: a philosophical view wherein individuals fail to find objective meaning in life; for the existentialist, life's meaning is subjectively tied to the freedom of each individual.

Hedonism: an ethical approach wherein the individual bases his or her actions upon what might produce the greatest amount of pleasure.

Incompatibilism: the approach to free will that asserts man is free only if he has the ability to choose a course of action or to do otherwise.

Motivational: that which influences one to act; used with reference to an ethical approach that provides sufficient reason to act appropriately.

Objective: independent of man's ideas; used with reference to an ethical approach that is not subject to man's interpretation.

Relativism: the idea that truth is dependent upon the perspective of the individual. This philosophy asserts that there is more than one correct way to view things.

Situationism: an ethical approach that holds that the means necessary to accomplish an action can be justified so long as the aforementioned means are based on love; each case is dependent upon the situation.

Teleological: the approach to ethics that is concerned primarily with the end result.

Utilitarianism: an ethical approach wherein individuals seek the greatest good for the greatest number of people over time.

Endnotes

Chapter 1

1 Wallace I. Matson, *A New History of Philosophy: From Thales to Ockham,* vol. 1 (San Diego: Harcourt, 1987) 68.

2 William F. Lawhead, *The Voyage of Discovery: A Historical Introduction to Philosophy* (Belmont: Wadsworth, 2002) 31.

3 Solomon's statement is similar to that found in Paul's sermon on Mars' Hill describing how men should "seek the Lord, in the hope that they might grope for Him and find Him" (Acts 17:27).

4 Adam Clarke, *Clarke's Commentary,* vol. 1 (Nashville: Abingdon, 1977) 38.

5 René Descartes, *Descartes Selections,* ed. Ralph M. Eaton (New York: Scribner's, 1955) 96.

Chapter 2

1 Claude A. Villee, Warren F. Walker Jr., and Robert D. Barnes, *General Zoology* (Fort Worth: Saunders College, 1984) 11.

2 Wayne Jackson, *The Human Body: Accident or Design?* (Stockton: Courier, 2000) 19-20.

3 William Paley, *Natural Theology* 9-16, qtd. in J.W. Monser, *An Encyclopedia on the Evidences: Or Masterpieces of Many Minds* (Nashville: Gospel Advocate, 1961) 113.

4 Villee 432.

5 Clarke 42.

6 This reproductive principle is mentioned in five verses in Genesis 1 (vv. 11-12, 21, 24-25).

7 For a thorough discussion about proofs for the Bible's inspiration, see chapter 8 of Chad Ramsey, *Reasons to Believe: A Survey of Christian Evidences* (Nashville: Gospel Advocate, 2008).

Chapter 3

1 Charles Hodge, *Systematic Theology,* vol. 2 (1871; Peabody: Hendrickson, 2003) 46.

2 C.F. Keil and F. Delitzsch, *Commentary on the Old Testament,* vol. 10 (1866; Peabody: Hendrickson, 2006) 605.

3 C.S. Lewis, *The Problem of Pain* (New York: Macmillan, 1978) 147.

4 The idea that God created anything because He *needed* to do so seems tenuous in light of Paul's address to the philosophers in Athens (Acts 17:24-25).

5 John Mark Hicks, *Yet Will I Trust Him: Understanding God in a Suffering World* (Joplin: College Press, 2000) 283.

6 Guy N. Woods, *Questions and Answers: Open Forum,* vol. 2 (Nashville: Gospel Advocate, 2001) 233.

7 Earl D. Edwards, *1 and 2 Thessalonians (Truth for Today Commentary)* (Searcy: Resource, 2008) 192.

Chapter 4

1 James Burton Coffman, *Commentary on Luke* (Abilene: ACU, 1984) 67.

2 Hicks 33.

3 Lionel Ruby, *Logic: An Introduction* (Cresskill: Paper Tiger, 2000) 131.

4 Thomas B. Warren, *Logic and the Bible* (Moore: National Christian, 1994) 14.

5 Roderick M. Chisholm, *Theory of Knowledge* (Englewood Cliffs: Prentice Hall, 1966) 105.

6 James D. Bales, "We Can Know the Truth," *The Spiritual Sword* 1.1 (Oct. 1969): 6-7.

Chapter 5

1 George Herbert Livingston, *Genesis, Beacon Bible Commentary,* vol. 1 (Kansas City: Beacon Hill, 1969) 41.

2 Aristotle, *Politics* 1252 b 26-29, trans. C.D.C. Reeve (Indianapolis: Hackett, 1998) 30.

3 Aristotle 1253 a 3-4, 30.

4 Frederick Copleston, *A History of Philosophy*, vol. 1 (New York: Doubleday, 1993) 351.

5 Matthew Henry, *Matthew Henry's Commentary on the Whole Bible*, vol. 3 (1710; Old Tappan: Revell, 1983) 949.

6 Thomas B. Warren, *Your Marriage Can Be Great*, ed. Thomas B. Warren (Jonesboro: National Christian, 1978) 195.

7 John Donne, "For Whom the Bell Tolls," *The Treasure Chest*, ed. Charles L. Wallis (San Francisco: Harper and Row, 1965) 41.

Chapter 6

1 Thomas Reid, "Nonnaturalism: Intuitive Knowledge of Ethical Facts," *The Problems of Philosophy*, ed. William P. Alston and Richard B. Brandt (Boston: Allyn and Bacon, 1974) 150.

2 Kelly James Clark and Anne Poortenga, *The Story of Ethics: Fulfilling Our Human Nature* (Upper Saddle River: Prentice Hall, 2003) 12.

3 Clark and Poortenga 158.

4 C.S. Lewis, *Mere Christianity* (1952; New York: Touchstone, 1996) 18.

5 Norman L. Geisler, *Christian Ethics: Options and Issues* (Grand Rapids: Baker, 1989) 25.

6 Lewis, *Mere Christianity* 18.

7 Gordon Graham, *Eight Theories of Ethics* (New York: Routledge, 2004) 20.

8 Louis P. Pojman, *Ethics: Discovering Right and Wrong* (Belmont: Wadsworth, 1990) 59.

9 Geisler 51.

10 Batsell Barrett Baxter, *I Believe Because: A Study of the Evidence Supporting Christian Faith* (Grand Rapids: Baker, 1971) 250.

11 Geisler 20.

12 Graham 178.

13 Clark and Poortenga 66-67.

14 Lawhead 342-43.

15 Reid 150.

16 Plato, "Euthyphro" 10 a, *The Collected Dialogues of Plato*, ed. Edith Hamilton and Huntington Cairns (Princeton: Princeton, 1996) 178.

17 Graham 188.

18 William K. Frankena, "Reasons for Acting Morally," *The Problems of Philosophy*, ed. William P. Alston and Richard B. Brandt (Boston: Allyn and Bacon, 1974) 247-48.

Chapter 7

1 J.A.C. Fagginger Auer and Julian Hartt, *Humanism Versus Theism* (Ames: Iowa State, 1981) 40.

2 Harold S. Kushner, *When Bad Things Happen to Good People* (New York: Anchor, 2004) 72-73.

3 Guy N. Woods, *A Commentary on the New Testament Epistles of Peter, John and Jude* (Nashville: Gospel Advocate, 1970) 256.

4 David Lipscomb, *Salvation From Sin* (Nashville, Gospel Advocate, 1950) 178.

5 Brad Harrub and Bert Thompson, *The Truth About Human Origins* (Montgomery: Apologetics Press, 2003) 463.

Chapter 8

1 Bill Flatt, "Sexual Counseling," *Personal Counseling: A Guide for Christian Counselors and Help for Individuals in Working Through Personal Family Problems Toward Positive Solutions*, ed. Bill Flatt (Searcy: Resource, 1991) 188-89.

2 Augustine, "On the Good of Marriage," *Nicene and Post-Nicene Fathers,* vol. 3, ed. Philip Schaff (Peabody: Hendrickson, 2004) 403.

3 Robert P. George, *In Defense of Natural Law* (New York: Oxford, 2001) 141.

4 H. Leo Boles, qtd. in Guy N. Woods, *Questions and Answers: Open Forum,* vol. 1 (Henderson: Freed-Hardeman, 1976) 299.

5 Martel Pace, *Hebrews (Truth for Today Commentary)* (Searcy: Resource, 2007) 559.

6 Daniel Akin, *God on Sex: The Creator's Ideas About Love, Intimacy, and Marriage* (Nashville: B and H, 2003) 3.

7 Ted Burleson, *Marriage and the Christian Home* (Haleyville: Riddle Creek, 2008) 68.

8 Burleson 68.

9 Akin 3.

10 Geisler 274.

11 Donald S. Metz, *1 Corinthians, Beacon Bible Commentary,* vol. 8 (Kansas City: Beacon Hill, 1968) 369.

Chapter 9

1 Kerry Duke, *God at a Distance* (Huntsville: Publishing Designs, 1995) 15-16.

2 William L. Rowe, *Philosophy of Religion: An Introduction* (Belmont: Wadsworth, 2001) 148.

3 John Calvin, qtd. in *Cyclopedia of Biblical, Theological, and Ecclesiastical Literature,* vol. 2, ed. John McClintock and James Strong (Grand Rapids: Baker, 1968) 42-43.

4 Manuel Velasquez, *Philosophy: A Text With Readings* (Belmont: Wadsworth, 1999) 236.

5 D.A. Carson, *How Long, O Lord?: Reflections on Suffering and Evil* (Grand Rapids: Baker, 2006) 213.

6 William J. Abraham, *An Introduction to the Philosophy of Religion* (Englewood Cliffs: Prentice Hall, 1985) 143.

7 Abraham 147.

8 Rowe 150.

9 Duke 18.

10 Thomas B. Warren, *Have Atheists Proved There Is No God?: A Critical Study of the Strongest Argument Which Has Been Advanced in Favor of Atheism* (Moore: National Christian, 1994) 69.

11 Karl Menninger, *Whatever Became of Sin?* (New York: Hawthorn, 1975) 19.

12 Carson 40.

13 Alvin Plantinga, *God, Freedom, and Evil* (Grand Rapids: Eerdmans, 1977) 30.

Chapter 10

1 Duke 104.

2 Carol K. Sigelman and David R. Shaffer, *Life-Span Human Development* (Pacific Grove: Brooks/Cole, 1995) 295-96.

3 Duke 103.

4 Eddie Cloer, *Psalms 1-50 (Truth for Today Commentary)* (Searcy: Resource, 2004) 586.

5 Wayne Jackson, *The Bible and Mental Health* (Stockton: Courier, 1998) 6.

6 Billy J. Watson, "Counseling Angry Persons," *Personal Counseling: A Guide for Christian Counselors and Help for Individuals in Working Through Personal Family Problems Toward Positive Solutions,* ed. Bill Flatt (Searcy: Resource, 1991) 91.

7 Paul L. Cates, "Counseling Anxious Persons," *Personal Counseling: A Guide for Christian Counselors and Help for Individuals in Working Through Personal Family Problems Toward Positive Solutions,* ed. Bill Flatt (Searcy: Resource, 1991) 79.

8 Henry Ward Beecher, qtd. in Charles H. Spurgeon, *The Treasury of David,* vol. 1 (Peabody: Hendrickson, 2008) 357.

9 Charles L. Allen, *God's Psychiatry* (Old Tappan: Revell, 1953) 39.

10 Hugo McCord, *Happiness Guaranteed* (Murfreesboro: Dehoff, 1956) 8.

11 Charles R. Brewer, *Be Not Dismayed: Messages of Cheer and Lessons of Truth* (Nashville: Gospel Advocate, 1958) 34.

Chapter 11

1 Lewis M. Hopfe and Mark R. Woodward, *Religions of the World* (Upper Saddle River: Prentice Hall, 2004) 6.

2 George L. Abernathy and Thomas A. Langford, *Philosophy of Religion* (New York: Macmillan, 1964) 1.

3 James Thrower, *Religion: The Classical Theories* (Washington: Georgetown, 1999) 4.

4 Hopfe and Woodward 5-6.

5 James Burton Coffman and Thelma B. Coffman, *Ecclesiastes, Song of Solomon, Lamentations* (Abilene: ACU, 1993) 28.

6 Moses E. Lard, *A Commentary on Romans* (Delight: Gospel Light, 1945) 52.

Chapter 12

1 David Stewart, *Exploring the Philosophy of Religion* (Upper Saddle River: Prentice Hall, 2001) 86.

2 Abraham 201.

3 Robert M. Veatch, "Defining Death Anew," *Life and Death: A Reader in Moral Problems*, ed. Louis P. Pojman (Belmont: Wadsworth, 2000) 208.

4 David J. Mayo and Daniel Winkler, "Euthanasia and the Transition From Life to Death," *Life and Death: A Reader in Moral Problems*, ed. Louis P. Pojman (Belmont: Wadsworth, 2000) 229.

5 Carson 97.

6 Emily Dickinson, "The Chariot," *The Treasure Chest*, ed. Charles L. Wallis (San Francisco: Harper and Row, 1965) 143.

7 Wilbur M. Smith, *Therefore Stand* (Grand Rapids: Baker, 1945) 367.

8 Abraham 211.

Chapter 13

1 Rudolf Bultmann, "elpis," Theological Dictionary of the New Testament, vol. 2, ed. Gerhard Kittel (Grand Rapids: Eerdmans, 2006) 522.

2 Søren Kierkegaard, "Either/Or," *A Kierkegaard Anthology*, ed. Robert Bretall (New York: Modern Library, 1946) 26.

3 Jean-Paul Sartre, "Existentialism," *Issues in Christian Thought*, ed. John B. Harrington (New York: McGraw-Hill, 1968) 382.

CPSIA information can be obtained at www.ICGtesting.com
Printed in the USA
LVOW10s0713221215

467459LV00001B/5/P